The Order of Chaos, or
The Essentials of Book Collecting

by

Richard Russell

Sangraal Books   Tempe, AZ
2009

Copyright Sangraal, Inc., 2009

All rights reserved

.

The Order of Chaos,
or the Essentials of Book Collecting

Bibliomania is a clinical disorder, thus book collecting is the only hobby that is also a mental disorder and about the only field of academic interest that requires a madman to understand it. I have often thought book collecting as an exercise in ordo res vacuus ordo, bad Latin for the order of things that have no order or the order of chaos. And it is probably bad form to admit a mental disorder to open a reference book. Unfortunately, it is the only possible admission in this field that firmly establishes the credibility of the author.

Those of us who chose to handle our pathology by becoming booksellers, perhaps aggravate the situation in that we have made our place in the world by buying what we cannot afford or understand and selling what we would rather keep. And yet, in the final analysis such irrationality may be the only way in which this field can be fully understood.

The first edition is the prime example of the irrationality of the field. In most cases the first edition of any book is the poorest example of it. As a book goes through successive printings, errors are found and remedied. So as the book itself actually improves, its collectability diminishes. And yet there is a certain thrill to be felt holding in your hands the very first appearance in the world of a piece of literature, the first mention of certain facts, the first time words were put together just that way. And as it sits book collecting hinges on that emotion, not on a firm basis of fact.

No book really covers all the things that have to be touched on to build a book collection of any value. Each subject gets references scattered here and there. While I put more publishers in my first edition section, more pseudonyms in my pseudonym dictionary, more terms in my glossary, than any other book or collection currently provides, before it is printed a dozen people will start publishing companies and two dozen pseudononymous authors will sign hundreds of books, while a talented printer invents a new technique or designs a new typeface. The difference in what I'm doing is not to cover all of it; printing is not accomplished fast enough to do that for even a day, assuming it could be done at all. The object is really to cover all the fields as compactly as possible so that in a very large percentage of cases, the book is all that you need to determine whether or not a book is considered collectible and how you would describe that.

What you need to know to collect books is the basic language of book collecting, how to distinguish editions, who the authors are (or at least pretending to be), a reason to collect and bibliographic facts of collectible books. All of which is absurd in that a book is collectible if it is collected. Most authors, I expect, hope it will be the tenth printing that is collectible, in that most books don't even have a second.

Part One

Learn the Language

A Basic Listing

A book listing is basically the same from a bookseller as from an academic or a librarian, though it should be admitted that the two are not in any way the same in outlook or, for the most part in methodology. This is I expect, a hang over from mankind's ancient heritage in that academics and librarians are gatherers, while book collectors and booksellers are hunters. In any case, a book listing is constructed:

Author. Title. Place: Publisher, Date.

Why? I don't know. The important thing to remember about it is that a knowledgable bookseller lists books this way and if you see one that doesn't match it is a good idea to double check everything twice before buying.

Basic Glossary

Learning the terms of book collecting will save you time and money. Of course that isn't always the major criteria. However, it is still in the mix. If one is insane enough to enter the field, the insanity should be enjoyed, savored. In no way should it be an insanity that you suffer from.

Advance Reading Copy- Abbreviated ARC. A copy distributed to reviewers, and/or the book trade previous to publication (See also: Uncorrected Proof).

association copy- A book given to an acquaintance prominent person by the Author, signed or unsigned.

back matter- pages following text

bands- 1) Cords on which a book is sewn 2) ridges across the spine of a leather-bound book.

belles lettres- Literature written for purposes of art, usually poetry essays and the like.

beveled boards- Books bound on boards with slanting (beveled) edges.

bibliography- 1) the technique of describing books academically 2) the science of books. 3) a book containing and cataloguing other books by author, subject, publisher etc.

blind stamp- embossed impression on a book cover without ink or gilt.

boards- hardbound book covers

bookplate- Ownership label in a book.

book sizes-

atlas folio	16" X 25"
elephant folio	14" X 23"
folio	12" X 15"
4to (quarto)	9" X 12"
8vo (octavo)	6" X 9"
12mo (duodecimo)	5" X 71/2"
16mo (Sextodecimo)	41/4" X 63/4"
18mo (Vicesimo-quarto)	4" X 61/4"
24 mo (Tricesimo)	31/2" X 6"

bosses- metal ornamentations on a book cover.

broadside- printed on one side only.

buckram- heavy cloth used in book binding.

cancels- Any part of the book that has been replaced for the original printing, usually to replace defective leaves.

chapbook- small format, cheaply made book.

codex- manuscript book, or book printed from a hand written manuscript

colophon- A device used by printers and publishers to identify themselves, like a crest. Used by some publishers to designate a first edition.

copyright- literally the right to copy or publish

copyright page- reverse of the title page, also called the "verso".

curiosa- books of unusual subject matter generally used for occult books and sometimes as a euphemism for erotica dedication- honorary inscription by an author printed with a literary work

deposit copy- copy of the book deposited in the national library to secure copyright.

detent- blind stamp used on rear board to designate a book club edition.

endpapers- papers preceding and following the front matter, text and back matter of a book.

erotica- books dealing with sexual matters.

ex-library/ex libris- a book formerly in a library/books formerly owned usually followed by the owner's or former owner's name.

facsimile- exact copy or reproduction

first edition- First appearance of a work, for the most part, independently, between it's own covers.

first printing- Product of the initial print run of a work, is either a "First Edition", or "First Thus".

first issue- Synonymous with "First Edition".

first impression- Synonymous with "First Edition".

flexible binding- 1) a binding of limp material, usually leather 2) a binding technique that allows a new book to lie flat while open

foreword- same as introduction

format- Basically the number of times the printed original is folded: Folio- once. Quarto- twice. Octavo- thrice. Duodecimo- four times. Sextodecimo- Five times. Vicesimo-quarto- six times. Tricesimo- seven times.

foxing- age darkening of paper, also called "age toning"

free end paper- blank page(s) between endpaper and front and back matter.

front matter- pages preceding text.

half-binding- Usually used with leather as "half-leather" or cloth as "half cloth. spine and corners are in leather or cloth.

head band- 1) small band of cloth inside the back of the spine of a book 2) decorative illustration or photo at the head of a page or chapter

imprimatur- a license to publish where censorship exists

imprint- 1) publisher's name 2) printer's name

in print- book is available new.

incunabula- books produced before 1501.

interleaved- blank pages added to book for notes etc,

introduction- preliminary text, also called foreword

jacket- printed or unprinted paper wrapped around a book also called dust jacket or dust wrapper.

leaves- single pages of a bound book

library binding- endpapers as well as first and last signatures reinforced and smythe sewn.

limited edition- a single edition for which only a limited number of copies are printed before the printing plates are destroyed

marginalia- notes printed in the margin

n.d- no date- indicates the book has no date of publication or copyright

n.p. no place- indicates a book has no printed place of publication

nihil obstat - indicates a book has the sanction of the Roman Catholic Church

o.p. Out of print- book is no longer available new

P.B.O./PBO Paperback original

pirate(d) edition- book issued without the consent of the copyright holder, usually in another country

 points - Additions, deletions or errors that result in identifying points.

plates- illustration printed on special paper and bound with the book

posthumous- published after the author's death

private press- publisher, usually small and specialized

pseudonym- pen name or false name used by an author

quarter binding- spine covered in cloth or leather

recto- right hand page usually used to refer to the title page.

rebind- a book rebound from the original

reback- quarter bind over original binding

remainder- publisher's overstock sold cheaply

remainder mark- any marking used to identify a remaindered book

reprint- all printings after the first

review copy- gratis copy of a book sent out for review

rubricated- printed in red and black

signature- a folded printed sheet ready for sewing and binding 2) a letter or number placed on the first page of a signature as a binding guide

slip-case- a box manufactured to hold a particular book

state- A change that occurs during a print run. Such as the correction of a typo, or a change in the binding or dust jacket

tip in- a leaf added on a single page, or glued to a blank page.

title page- page which gives the title author publisher etc. referred to as the "recto"

unauthorized edition- same as pirate edition

uncorrected proof- book issued before the final edit usually used as an advance reading copy or review copy

uncut- leaves that have not been machine cut

unopened- folded edges that have not been cut.

vanity press- a publisher subsidized by the author

variant- Points or states without a known priority.

verso- left hand page identified with the copyright page.

woodcut- engraving printed from a carved block of wood

wormed- insect damaged

wrapper- separate jacket, or the covers of a paperbound book.

xlibris or x-libris- formerly owned, usually accompanied by a name or institution.

Grading Terms

When you can't hold a book in your hands before buying, and even with the reach of the Internet it is often impossible to do so, a competent bookseller will describe its condition to you. This often leads to violent disagreement and is somewat hard to fathom. Nonetheless it is the only way there is to bridge an emotional gap with words, so poor as it is, it is the standard.

The first thing to determine in grading a book is the tightness of the binding. This shows the overall wear of the book and, presumably, how often it has been read. To do this place the book on it's spine and open so that the covers stand at a 45 degree angle and let go.

If the book closes completely, the initial grade is fine

If the book closes and the cover doesn't, the initial grade is near fine.

If the book opens and the pages fan, the initial grade is very good.

If the book lies flat open to a page, the book is, at best, good.

Some booksellers deviate here. A fine book may be downgraded to near fine or even very good due to other flaws such as foxing, dog-eared pages, notes in the text and other factors. My own preference, and that followed by a good many used booksellers, is to begin with the objective standard above, and note the other problems separately.

below these grades are:

Fair- a good book that is severely worn

Poor- a book that is falling apart but readable.

Either of these two grades might also be called a reading copy.

A binding copy is a book that cannot be read as it is falling apart but is whole and can be rebound into an acceptable book.

I have seen many different conventions for grading books. Most are filled with ambiguous terms such as "crisp". For many years I have recommended the objective system above. Either because I like to be able to test something, or because I am just too dense to understand what "crisp" means when applied to a book and not an apple.

However, to cover all bases, in 1949, *AB Bookman* rewrote its grading standards so that the basic terms would be more encompassing. This is the 1949 AB Bookman Standard:

As New is to be used only when the book is in the same immaculate condition in which it was published. There can be no defects, no missing pages, no library stamps, etc., and the dustjacket (if it was issued with one) must be perfect, without any tears. (The term As New is preferred over the alternative term Mint to describe a copy that is perfect in every respect, including jacket.)

Fine approaches the condition of As New, but without being crisp. For the use of the term Fine there must also be no defects, etc., and if the jacket has a small tear, or other defect, or looks worn, this should be noted.

Very Good can describe a used book that does show some small signs of wear (but no tears) on either binding or paper. Any defects must be noted.

Good describes the average used and worn book that has all pages or leaves present. Any defects must be noted.

Fair is a worn book that has complete text pages (including those with maps or plates) but may lack endpapers, half-title, etc. (which must be noted). Binding, jacket (if any), etc. may also be worn. All defects must be noted.

Poor describes a book that is sufficiently worn that its only merit is as a Reading Copy because it does have the complete text, which must be legible. Any missing maps or plates should still be noted. This copy may be soiled, scuffed, stained or spotted and may have loose joints, hinges, pages, etc.

Ex-library copies must always be designated as such no matter what the condition of the book.

Book Club editions must always be noted as such no matter what the condition of the book.

Binding Copy describes a book in which the pages or leaves are perfect but the binding is very bad, loose, off, or nonexistent.

Identify First Editions

A general definition for a first edition is the first time that a written work appears in a separate cover. This is an elastic definition and can create some disagreement. To take an example:

Paso Por Aqui by Eugene Manlove Rhodes, is one of the most famous and sought after Western novels. Its first appearance was in the Saturday Evening Post in February of 1927. It was published as the second novel in *Once in the Saddle* by Houghton Mifflin shortly thereafter. It was republished by Houghton Mifflin in 1949 in *The Best Novels and Short Stories of Eugene Manlove Rhodes*. The first edition of *Paso Por Aqui*, by the definition above, is by the University of Oklahoma, in 1973. However, if you can find *Once in the Saddle* in the first printing, you have a book worth, depending on condition, from $500. to $1000. The University of Oklahoma "first" is worth from $25. to $50.

So, when you say, "first edition" you are basically talking about the first appearance of a piece of writing in book form. Ideally, you want the first printing, the first state, complete as it was issued (with errata slips, dust jacket etc.) This is important to the collector in the same way an original painting is important to an art collector. It represents the first appearance in the real world of the piece of writing.

Of course it is also, most likely, the worst state of any book. And often the most valuable and collectible book can be identified by the errors it contains in printing, editing, and binding.

While it can be said each publisher has a unique way of marking first editions, there are some basic methods:

1) The date on the title page matches the copyright date, and no additional printings are listed on the verso (copyright page).
2) The verso does not list additional printings.
3) "First Edition", "First Printing"," First Impression", "First Issue" or a variation of these printed on the title page or verso.
4) "First Published (date)" or "Published (date)" on the verso
5) A colophon (publishers logo) printed on the title page, verso or at the end of the book.
Simply follow these numbers on the chart.

A printers code, basically a line of numbers or letters printed on the verso, showing a "1" or an A at one end or the other, with certain variations (explanation follows the chart.) If the book has an ISBN number check this first, though it only shows the publisher's print run and doesn't validate the edition.

There are also unique methods that are exclusive to a single publisher or only two or three publishers (explanation and list follows the chart.)

Publisher	1	2	3	4	5	Reprint Reprint Publisher
101 Productions		x				
A.A.Wyn, Inc.	x					
A & C Black LTD	before 1947		after 1947			
A & C Black Limited				x		
A.H. & A. W. Reed		x				
A. Kroch & Son		x				
Adam and Charles Black			x			
A.C.McClurg & Co.				x		
A.S.Barnes & Co. Inc,		x				
A. L. Burt						x
A. R. Mowbray		x				
ABC (All Books for Children)				x		
Abelard-Schuman, Ltd.				x		
Abington Press		x				x
Academic Press		x				
Academy Chicago		x				
Ace			x			
Ace/Putnam		x				
Acropolis Books		x				
ACS		x				
Adam Hilger		x				
Adastra Press					x	
Adirondack Mountain Club		x				
Advocado Press		x				
Ashanta Press		x				
Airlife Publishing				x		
Aivia Press			x			
Alan Sutton				x		
Alan Swallow, Publisher	x			x		
Alan Wolfsy		x				
Alaska		x				

Northwest						
Alabatross Books			x			
Alan R. Liss		x				
Albert & Charles Boni		x				
Albert and Charles Boni	x					
Albert Whitman	x					
Albyn Press				x		
Aletheia Publishing			x			
Alfred Publishing		x				
Alfred A, Knopf Inc.	x	x	x			
Alliance Book Corporation	x					
ALICEJAMES Books		x				
Allan Wingate				x		
Allen A. Knoll		x				
Allen D. Bragdon.		x				
Allen Publishing		x		x		
Alpha Beat Press		x				
Altamount Press			x			
Altermus						x
Alyson Publications			x			
Amber Lane Press		x		x		
American Bar Foundation		x				
American Catholic Press		x				
American Library Association		x				
American Publishing Company	x	x				
Amphoto		x				
Anchorage Press		x				
Ancient City Press			x			
Anderson Press				x		

Andrew Dakers				x		
Andrews and McMeel			x			
Andre Deutsch				x		
Angus and Robertson				x		
Antique Collector's Club			x	x		
Antonson Publishing			x			
Anvil Press		x				
Aperture			x			
Appletree Press		x				
Applezaba Press		x				
Aquarian Press				x		
Arcadia House	x					
Architectual Book Publishing		x				
Architectual Press				x		
Archway Press		x				
Arco Publishing Co. Inc	x					
Arden Press		x				
Argus Books	x					
Argus Book Shop		x				
Ariel Press			x			
Arion Press		x				
Arizona Silhouettes	x					
Arkham House		x				
Arlen House				x		
Arlington House		x				
Art and Education Publishers				x		
Art Institute of Chicago		x				
Artabras			x			
Arthur Baker				x		
Arthur H. Clark		x				
Asher-Gallant		x				
Ashgrove Press				x		

Ashmolean Museum	x	x			
Ashton Scholastic		x			
Aspen Publishers		x			
Associated University Presses		x			
Asylum Arts		x			
Atheneum Publishers			x		
Atlantic Monthly Press (after 1925);	x		x		
Auckland University Press				x	
Avalon Press				x	
Ave Maria Press		x			
Avenel						x
Avon			x		
B.T.Batsford				x	
B.W.Dodge & Company		x			
B.W.Huebach		x			
Baachus Press			x		
Background Books				x	
Bailey Bros. & Swinfin		x			
Baker & Taylor		x			
Baker House		x			
Bancroft-Sage		x			
Banner of Truth Trust				x	
Banyan Books		x			
Barlenmir House			x		
Barn Owl Books				x	
Barnard & Westwood		x			
Barre Publishing Company Inc.		x			
Barricade Books			x		
Bartholomew Books		x			

Basil Blackwell		x				
Basil Blackwell and Mott (Basil Blackwell Limited)				x		
Battery Press		x				
Baylor University		x				
BBC Books				x		
Beach Holme			x			
Beacon Press	x					
Beautiful America			x			
Beechhurst Press		x				
Beehive Press		x				
Behrman House		x				
Being Publications		x				
Ben Abramson	x					
Bergh Publishing		x				
Bergin & Garvey				x		
Berkshire House			x			
Bern Potter			x			
Bernard Geis Associates			x			
Bernard's LTD				x		
Bess Press		x				
Better Homes and Gardens			x			
Bhaktivedanta Book Trust			x			
Bicycle Books		x				
Big Sky			x			
Big Table			x			
Birch Brook Press			x			
Black Lace				x		
Black Swan			x			
Black Tie Press			x			
Black's Reader's Service						x
Blackie & (and) Son		before 1957		after 1957		
Blackwell		x				

Scientific						
Blakiston						x
Blanford Press				x		
Bloch Publishing		x				
Bloodaxe Books				x		
Blue Dove Press			x			
Blue Ribbon Books						x
Blue Star						x
Blue Wind Press		x				
Boa Editions			x			
Bobbs-Merrill Company			x		Before 1936	
The Bodley Head				x		
Bolchazy-Carducci		x				
Boni & Gaer Inc.	x	x				
Boni & Liveright		x	fitfully			
The Book Guild Limited		x		x		
Books West Southwest	x					
The Borgo Press			x			
Bottom Dog Press		x				
Boxwood Press		x				
Boydell & Brewer				x		
Boydell Press				x		
Boyds Mills						
Bracken Books						x
Bradt Publications			before 1989	after 1989		
The Branden Press		x				
Brentano's	before 1927		after 1927			
Brewer & Warren	x	x				
Brewer, Warren and Putnam	x	x				
Brewin Books					x	
Brick Row			x	x		

Bridge	+ Code 1-10					
British Academy		x				
British Library				x		
British Museum				x		
British Museum Press				x		
Broadside Press			x			
Brockhampton Press		x				
Brompton Books		x				
Bronx County Historical Society		x				
Brooke House		x				
Brookings Institute		x				
Brooklyn Botanic Garden		x				
Brown, Son & Ferguson			x			
Bruccoli Clark Layman			x			
Bruce Humphries, Inc.	x				x	
Bruce Publishing (Milwaukee, WI)		x				
Bulfinch Press			x			
Bull Run of Vermont		x				
Burgess & Wickizer			x			
Burke Publishing				x		
Burning Cities		x				
Burning Deck		x				
Burns & Mac Eachern		x				
Burns, Oates & Washbourne			After 1937	Before 1937		
Bush Press			x			
Butterworth & Co.		x				
Butterworth-				x		

Heinemann						
Butterworth Scientific				x		
Butterworths				x		
Butterworths PTY		x				
C. & J. Temple				x		
C.M.Clarke Publishing Co.		x				
C. V. Mosby		x				
C. W. Daniel				x		
Caddo Gap		x				
Cadmus Editions			x			
Calder Publications			x			
California Institute of Public Affairs		x				
California State University Press		x				
Cambridge University Press (UK & Australia)			x			
Cambridge University Press (North America)				x		
Camden House			x			
Camelot			x			
Cameron Associates	x					
Camino E.E. & Book Co.		x				
Canada Law Book		x				
Canterbury University Press				x		
Capra		x				
Captain Fiddle			x			
Caratzas Brothers		x				
Carcanet New Press				x		
Cardoza			x			
Carnegie Mellon			x			
Carolina		x				

Academic Press					
Carolina Wren Press		x			
Carolrhoda Books		x			
Carriage House					x
Carpenter Press			x		
Carstens		x			
Cassell & Co.		before 1976		after 1976	
Cassell LTD				x	
Cassell Publishers/ PLC				x	
Castalia Bookmakers		x			
Castle Books		x		x	
Catholic University Press of America		x			
Causeway Press Limited			x		
Cave Books		x			
Caxton Printers		x			
Cecil Palmer			x		
Cedar Bay Press			x		
Celestial Arts			x		
Centaur Press LTD		x			
Center for Afro-American Studies			x		
Center for Japanese Studies		x			
Center for Western Studies			x		
Centerstream			x		
Century (UK)				x	
Century Benham				x	
Century Company (US)	Fitfully				
Century Hutchinson				x	
Chapman & Hall		x			

Charles Knight				x	
Charles L. Webster and Company		x			
Charles Scribner's Sons (before 1929)	before 1929	before 1929			
Chariot			x		
Charles Press		x			
Charles River		x			
Charles T. Branford		x			
Charleton Press		x			
Chaterson Limited	x				
Chatham Press			x		
Chatto & Windus		x			
Cheever			x		
Chelsea Green			x		
Cherrytree Press				x	
Chester R. Heck		x			
Chicago Review			x		
Chilton		x			
China Books		x			
Christian Classics				x	
Christian Focus		x			
Christopher-Gordon			x		
Christopher Helm			x		
Christopher Helm Publishing LTD		x			
Christopher Johnson				x	
Christopher Publishing House		x			
Chronicle Books		x			
Cicerone Press		x			
Citadel Press		Before 1949	x		

		& after 1988			
City Lights		x			
Clarity Press		x			
Clarkson N. Potter Inc.			x		
Claude Kendall & Willoughby Sharp			x		
Claude Kendall Inc.			x		
Clearwater Publishing		x			
Cleaver-Hume				x	
Cliffhanger Press			x		
Cloud, Inc		x			
Cloudcap		x			
Coffee House		x			
Coldwater Press			x		
Colin Smythe				x	
Collier			x		Before 1989
Colonial Williamsburg Foundation		x			
Columbia University	x	x			
Commonwealth Press		x			
Conari Press			x		
Concordia		x			
Conservatory of American Letters		x			
Constable & Company				x	
Co-Operative Union LTD				x	
Copeland and Day		x			
Copper Beech		x			
Copper Canyon		x			
Cork University Press				x	
Cornell Maritime Press		x			
Cornell University Press		x			

Cornerstone		x			
Cosmopolitan Book Corporation		x	after1 927		
Cottage Press			x		
Cottage Publications		x			
Council for British Archeology		x			
Country Life LTD				x	
Countryman Press		x			
Covici-Friede		x	x		
Covici-McGee			x		
Coward, McCann and Geohegan		x	x		
Coward-McCann Inc.		x	x	Before 1936	
Creative Age Press Inc.		x			
Creative Press	x				
Cressrelles				x	
Crossing Press		x			
Crossroad/Cont inuum		x			
Crossway Books (UK)			x		
Crown Publishers	x	x			
Culinary Arts			x		
Cupples & Leon					x
Curbstone			x		
Currency Press		x			
Cypress Press			x		
D. S. Brewer				x	
Dalkey Archive			x		
Dana-Estes		x			
Dartmouth Publications		x			
Darnell Corporation		x			
Darton, Longman & Todd				x	
David & Charles LTD		x			
David &		x			

Charles PLC						
David McKay Co. Inc.	x					
David R. Godine			x			
Davis-Poynter		x				
DAW Books			x			
Dawn Horse Press			x			
Dee-Jay Publications				x		
Delacorte Press			x			
Dembner Books		x				
Denlinger's		x				
Dennis Dobson				x		
Department of Primary Industries				x		
Depth Charge			x			
Deseret	x					
DeVorss		x				
Dharma		x				
Dial Press			x			
Dial Press (Lincoln MacVeagh)	x	x				
Diana Press		x				
Diane Publishing		x				
Didier		x				
Dietz Press	x					
Dillon Press		x				
Dimi Press			x			
Discovery		x				
Disney		x				
Dodd Mead & Co.	x	x				
Dodge Publishing Company			x			
Dog Ear Press			x			
Dolphin		x				
Donning			x			
Doral		x				
Dorial			x			
Dorling Kidersley		x				
Dorrance & Co.			x			
Dorsey Press			x			

Doubleday & Co.			x			
Doubleday Doran & Company			x			
Doubleday Page & Company		x	x			
Douglas West			x			
Dover						x
Down Home			x			
Downlander				x		
Dreenan Press		x				
Duell, Sloan and Pearce			x			
Duffield & Co.	x	x	Fitfully			
Duffield & Green	x	x	x			
Duke University	x					
Dumbarton Oaks		x				
Dunster House Bookshop	x	x				
Dustbooks			x			
E. M. Hale		x				
E.P.Dutton & Co. Inc.		x	x			
Eagle's View			x			
Eakin Press			x			
Earth Magic			x			
East Woods Press			x			
Eastern Press		x				
Eaton & Mains		x				
Ebury Press				x		
Ecco Press			x			
Eclipse		x				
Eden Press			x			
Eden Publishing		x				
Edgar Rice Burroughs			x			
Edinburgh University Press				x		
Edmund Ward		x				
Educational Technology			x			
Edward Arnold		x				
Edward J.	x	x				

Clode Inc.					
Eighth Mountain			x		
Eland Books					x
Eldon Press				x	
Elkin Matthews		x			
Ellicott Press		x			
Elliot Right Way		x			
Elliot Stock	x				
ELM Publications				x	
Emerson Books		x			
Empty Bowl		x			
Ensign Press		x			
Enterprise Publications		x			
Entwhistle Books			x		
EPM Publications			x		
Epworth Press			x		
Equinox Cooperative Press	x				
Eric Partridge LTD		x	x		
Ernest Benn	x			x	
Essex Institute		x			
ETC Publications		x			
Europa			x		
Evans Brothers				x	
Evanston		x			
Eveleigh Nash and Grayson				x	
Eyre & Spottiswoode				x	
F. S. Crofts			x		
F.Tennyson Neeley		x			
Faber & Faber				x	
Faber & Gwyer				x	
Fabian Society		x			
Fairchild Books		x		x	
Falcon Press				x	
Falmouth Publishing House, Inc.	x				

Famedram		x			
Fantasy Press					
Fantasy Publishing			x		
Far Corner			x	x	
Farrar & Rinehart Inc.			x		x
Farrar Straus & Cudahy			x		x
Farrar Straus and Giroux			x		x
Farrar Straus			x		x
Feminist Press			x		
Fenland Press					
Feral House			x		
Fernhurst				x	
Fiction Collective			x		
Fiction Library						x
Fields, Osgood & Co.		x			
The Figures		x			
Firebird Books				x	
Fithian Press		x			
Fjord Press			x		
Fleming H. Revell Company		x			
Flyleaf Press		x			
Focal Press				x	
Follet Publishing Company			x		
Fordham University		x	x		
Forest Press	x				
Forum		x			
Forward Movement		x			
Four Seas Company	x				
Four Walls Eight Windows			x		
Frances Lincoln				After 1988	
Frances P. Harper	x	x			
Franciscan Press			x		
Franciscan University Press		x			

Frank Cass				x		
Frank Maurice		x				
Franklin Publishing		x				
Franklin Watts Inc.		x	x			
Frederic C. Beil			x	x		
Frederick Fell Publishers				x		
Frederick Muller				x		
Frederick Stokes & Co.	x	x			x	
Frederick Ungar		x				
Free Spirit		x				
Freedom Press		x				
Fromm International			x			
Funk & Wagnells Inc.				x		
G. Bell & Sons				x		
G. Howard Watt	x					
G.P.Putnam's Sons	x	x				
G.W.Carleton	x	x				
G.W.Dillingham Company		x		x		
G W Graphics		x				
Gaff Press			x			
Gambit			x			
Gambling Times		x				
Ganley			x			
Gannet			x			
Garamond Press		x				
Garber			x			
Gaslight		x	x			
Gay & Hancock		x				
Genealogical Publishing		x				
Geoffrey Bles				x		
Geoffrey Chapman				x		
George Allen & Unwin				x		
George Braziller Inc.			x			

George H. Doran & Co.			x		x	
George Harrap				x		
George Newnes		x	x			
George Routledge & Sons		x				
George Routledge & Sons, Kegan Paul, Trench,Trubner		x				
George Shumway			x			
George W. Stewart Publisher Inc.	x					
George Weidenfeld & Nicholson		x				
Geographical Association		x				
Gerald Duckworth				x		
Gerald Howe				x		
Gibbs Smith			x			
Gill and Macmillan		x				
Girl Scouts of America			x			
Glade House			x			
GLB Publishers			x			
Gleniffer Press			x			
Globe Pequot			x			
Globe Press			x			
Gnome Press			x			
Gnomon Press			After 1991			
Gold Eagle			x			
Golden West		x				
Golden West Historical Publications			x			
Goldsmith						x
Gollehon			After 1995			
Goose Lane		x				
Gordon Fraser Gallery				x		

Gower		x				
Grafton		x		x		
Granada		x		x		
Grant Richards		x				
Granta				x		
Graphic Arts Center		x				
Gray's		x				
Grayson & Grayson				x		
Graywolf				x		
Great Ocean			x			
Great Western		x				
Grebner Books			x			
Green Books			x			
Greenberg, Publisher, Inc.	x	x				
Greenfield Review			x			
Greenlawn Press		x				
Greenwich House						x
Greenwillow			x			
Greenwood				x		
Gresham Press		x				
Greville Press				x		
Grey Fox		x				
Grey Seal				x		
Grey Walls		x		x		
Greystone Press			x			
Grindstone Press		x				
Grosset & Dunlap						x
Grossman		x				
Grove Press			x			
Gryphon			x			
Guiness				x		
Gulf Publishing		x				
Gumbs & Thomas			x			
H.C. Kinsey & Company Inc.	x	x				
H.W.Wilson Company	x	x				
Halcyon Press				x		
Hale, Cushman & Flint		x				

Hamish Hamilton				x		
Hammond, Hammond & Co.		x				
Hampshire Bookshop		x				
Hancock House		x				
Hanging Loose Press		x				
Hannibal Books				x		
Harcourt Brace etc.			x	x		
Harper & Row			x			
Harper Collins			x			
Harper Collins PTY (Aust.)				x		
Harper Collins LTD (N.Z.)				x		
Harpswell			x			
Harrap Ltd				x		
Harrap Publishing				x		
Harrison Smith & Robert Haas Inc.	x	x	x			
Harrison Smith Inc.	x	x	x			
Harry Cuff		x				
Harvard Business School		x				
Harvard University Press	x	x				
Harvester Press				x		
Harvey Miller		x				
Hastings House Publishers, Inc.	x	Letterpress				
Hawthorn			x			
Haynes		x	x			
Heat Press			x			
Heath Cranton		x				
Heimburger House			x			
Heinemann New Zealand				x		
Hellman, Williams		x				

Hendrick-Long		x			
Henkle-Yewdale		x			
Henry Altemus		x			
Henry Holt & Co. Inc.	x		x	x	
Henry E. Huntington Library		x			
Henry Schumann Inc.	x	x			
Henry T. Coates & Co.				x	
Her Majesty's Stationary Office				x	
Herald Press (See unique)		x			
Herbert Jenkins		before 1948	after 1948		
Herbert Press				x	
Herbert S. Stone & Co.		x			
Hermes Publications			x		
Hermitage		x			
Hermitage House			x		
High-Lonesome Books			x		
Hill & Wang	x		x		
Hill of Content				x	
Hillman-Curl, Inc.	x				
Historic New Orleans			x		
H. Karnac LTD				x	
Hobby Horse		x			
Hodder & Stroughton				x	
Hoffman Press		x			
Hogarth Press	x	x			
Holiday House, Inc.		1947-1988	After 1988		
Hollis and Carter				x	
Holmes and Meier		x			
Holt Rinehart & Winston Inc.	x		x	x	

Homestead		Guideb ooks	x			
Hoover Institution		x				
Hope Publishing House		x				
Horace Liveright Inc.	x		x			
Horizon Press	x					
Horn Book		x				
Horwitz Grahame		x				
Houghton Mifflin Australia				x		
Houghton Mifflin Company				x		
House of Anansi		x				
Howard University		x				
Howe Brothers		x				
Howell-North		x				
Howell Press			x			
Howell Soskin Publishers	x					
Hudson Hills			x			
Hugh Evelyn				x		
Hull University		x				
Humanics Publishing			x			
Humanities Press		x				
Humanities Press International				x		
Huntington Library		x				
Hurst						x
Hurst & Blackett				x		
Hutchinson				x		
Hyperion		x				
I. E. Clark		x				
Ian Henry		x				
Icarus Press		x				
IDE House			x			
Ignatius Press		x				
Illuminated Way		x				

Images Australia PTY		x				
Impact		x				
Indiana Historical Society		x				
Indiana University Press	before 1974	after 1974				
Industrial Press			x			
Info Devil			x			
Inform		x				
Inner Traditions		x				
Institute of Education				x		
Institute of Jesuit Sources		Before 1993	After 1993			
Institute of Psychological Research		x				
Institute Chemical Engineers (UK)		x				
Institute of Electrical Engineers (UK)		x				
Intellect				x		
Intermedia Press		x				
International Publishers			x			
International Universities Press		x				
IOP Publishing		x				
Iowa State University Press	x					
IPD Enterprises				x		
Irish Academic Press		x				
Islamic Foundation		x				
Island Press (Australia)		x				
Island Press Cooperative		x				
IT Publications	x					
Italica Press				x		

Ives Washburn Inc.	x	x				
Ovor Nicholson & Watson			x			
J.A.Allen & Co.		x				
J.B.Lippencott Company			x	x		
J. Garnet Miller				x		
J. M. Dent & Sons		Before 1936		After 1936		
J. Michael Pearson		x				
J. Walter Black						x
J. Whittaker & Sons		x				
Jacaranda Press		x				
Jacaranda Wiley				x		
James & James				x		
James Duffy				x		
James M. Heineman		x				
James Nisbet		x	x			
James Pott	x					
James R. Osgood and Company		x				
Jane's Information Group			x			
Janus Press	x					
Jargon		x				
Jarolds		After 1948		Before 1948		
Jefferson House						
Jewish Publication Society	x		x			
John C.Winston Co.	x					
John Day		After 1937		Before 1937		
John F. Blair			x			
John Calder			x			
John Hamilton		x				
John Knox Press		x				

John Lane Company		x				
John Lane The Bodley Head LTD		Before 1928		After 1928		
John Long		x				
John Muir			x			
John Murray	Before 1982	After 1982				
John W. Luce & Company	x	x				
John Westhouse				x		
John Wiley & Sons		x				
Johns Hopkins University Press	x	x				
Jonathon Cape				x		
Jonathon Cape and Robert Ballou		x		Fitfully		
Jonathon Cape & Harrison Smith				x		
Jonathon David			x			
Jordan (s)		x				
Joseph J. Binns			x			
Journeyman Press				x		
Judson Press		x				
Julian Messner	x	x				
Juniper Press		x				
Junius-Vaughn			x			
Kalimat Press			x			
Kalmbach		x				
Kanchenjunga			x			
Kayak		x				
KC Publications		x				
Kegan Paul, Trench, Trubner & Co., LTD		x				
Kelsey St.		x				
Kensington			x			
Kent State University Press			x			
Kevin Weldon & Associates				x		

PTY					
Kindred		x			
King's Crown Press		x			
Kitchen Sink			x		
Kivaki Press			x		
Know Inc.			x		
Kodansha International			x		
L.C.Page & Co.			x	x	
Lacis		x			
Ladan			x		
Lahontian Images			x		
Lane Publishing			x		
Lansdowne Press				x	
Lantern Press, Inc.	x	x			
Lapis Press			x		
Larin			x		
Latimer House				x	
Lawrence and Wishart		x			
Lawrence Hill			x		
Lawrence J. Gomme		x			
Lea		x			
Lea & Febiger		x			
Lee and Shepard		x		x	
Legacy		x			
Leicester University Press				x	
Lennard Associates		x			
Leo Cooper				x	
Lerner Publications		x	x		
Levite of Apache			x		
Lewis Copeland Company				x	
Leyland		x	x		
Liberty Bell Press			x		
Liberty Fund		x			
Libra Press			x		

Library of America			Compi lati- ons			x
Lightning Tree		x	Sporat ic			
Liguori			After 1994			
Lillian Barber Press		x				
Limelight			x			x
Lindsay Drummond				x		
Literary Guild						x
Little Blue Books						x
Little Brown and Company		x	x			
Little Hills Press PTY LTD		x				
Liveright Publishing Corp.	x	x				
Liverpool University Press		x				
Livingston		x				
Llewellyn			x			
Log House		x				
Lone Eagle				x		
Longman, Inc.				x		
Longman Cheshire PTY				x		
Longmans Green & Co.		x	x			
Longstreet House		x				
Lord John Press			x			
Loring & Mussey, Inc.	x		x			
Lothrop Publishing Company	x	x				
Lothrop, Lee & Shepard Co. Inc.	x			x		
Louise Corteau, Editrice		x				
Louisiana State University Press	x	x				

Lovatt Dickson				x	
Luman Christi				x	
Lund Humphries				x	
Lutterworth				x	
Lynne Rienner		x			
M.Barrows & Company			x		
M. S. Mill		x			
Macaulay		x			
MacDonald				x	
MacFarland, Walter & Ross		x			
MacLay & Associates			x		
Macmillan Inc.		x	x		
Macrae-Smith Company			x		
Macy-Masius		x		x	
Mansell				x	
Marion Boyars Publishers, Inc.		x			
Marion Boyars Publishers. LTD				x	
Mark Zieseng			x		
Martin Brian & O'Keefe LTD				x	
Martin Secker & Warburg				After 1976	
Marshall Jones Company	x				
Martin Hopkinson	x	x		x	
Maryland State Archives		x			
Masquerade Books			x		
Matson					
Maurice Fridberg		x			
Maupin House			x		
Maxwell Droke		x			
May Davenport			x		
McClelland and Stewart		x			
McClure Phillips & Co		x		x	
McDowell Obolensky	x				

McGraw Hill Book Company	x		x		
McGraw Hill Ryerson		x			
McNally & Loftin, Publishers	x				
McPhee Gribble PTY				x	
McPherson			x		
Medici Society		Child & Art		x	
Melbourne University Press				x	
Memphis State University		x			
Mercat Press				x	
Mercer University Press		x			
Mercier Press		x			
Meredith Books			x		
Meridian Books		x			
Meridonal		x			
Meriwether			x		
Merlin Books LTD				x	
Merlin Press, Inc.		x			
Merriam-Webster			x		
Methuen				x	
Metropolitan Museum of Art		x			
Michael Haag			x		
Michael Joseph				x	
Michael Kesend			x		
Michell Kennerly		x			
Michigan State University Press		x			
Middle Atlantic Press			x		
Milestone				x	
Mills & Boon				x	
Minnesota	x				

Historical Society (after 1940)					
Minton Balch & Co,	x				
Missouri Archaelogical Press	x				
MIT Press	x				
MMB Music	x				
Mockingbird Books		x			
Modern Language Association	x				
Modern Library					x
Modern Age Books	x				
Moffat Yard and Company			x		
Mojave	x				
Monad Press		x			
Montana Historical Society	x				
Moody Press	After 1960				
Moon Publications		x			
Morehouse	x				
Morehouse-Barlow	x				
Morehouse-Graham	x				
Morgan & Lester	x				
Morgan & Morgan	x				
Morton		x			
Mosaic	x				
Mosby Yearbook	x				
Motorbooks			x		
Mountain Press	x				
Mountaineers Books		x			
Moutin de Gruyter	x				
Multimedia Publishing		x			
Murray &	x				

	Before 1981	After 1981			
McGee					
Museum of Modern Art		x			
Museum of New Mexico	Before 1981	After 1981			
Museum Press	x				
Mycroft & Moran		x			
Mysterious Press			x		
Mystery House		x			
Mystic Seaport Museum			x		
Nags Head Art			x		
Naiad Press			x		
National Foundation Press		x			
National Library of Australia		x			
National Library of Scotland				x	
National Museums of Scotland		x			
National Museum of Women in the Arts		x			
National Woodlands			x		
Nautical and Aviation		x			
Naylor		x			
Neale Publishing Company		x			
Nelson, Foster & Scott			x		
Nelson-Hall		x			
Netherlandic Press		x			
Neville-Spearman				x	
New American Library				x	
New Amsterdam			x		
New Classics					x
New Dawn			x		

New Directions		After 1976	After 1970		
New England Cartographics			x		
New England Press			After 1986		
New English Library				x	
New Harbinger		x			
New Native Press			x		
New Poets Series		x			
New Republic		x			
New South		x			
New South Wales University Press		x			
New Star			x		
New View		x			
New Woman's Press				x	
New York Culture Review			x		
New York Graphic Society			x		
New York Zoetrope			x		
Nine Muses		x			
Noel Douglas				x	
Nonesuch		x			
Noonday			x		
North Atlantic		x			
North Point Press		Before 1988			
North Star		x			
Northland			After 1972		
Northwestern University Press		x			
Northwoods Press		x			
Noyes, Platt & Company		x			
Oak Knoll		x			
Oakhill Press			x		
Oakwood Press		x			
Oasis Books				x	

Oberlin College Press			x			
O'Brien				x		
Ocean View			x			
Odyssey Press			x			
O'Hara		x				
Ohio State University Press	x					
Ohio University Press	x	x				
O'Laughlin			x			
Old Vicarage				x		
Oliver & Boyd			x			
Oliver Durrell		x				
OMF International				x		
Omnibus Books				x		
On Stream		x				
Open Court		x				
Open Hand			x			
Open University Press				x		
Orbis		x				
Oregon Historical Press		x				
Oregon State University Press		x				
Oriel Press		x				
O'Reilly and Associates		x				
Orion				x		
Otago		x				
Outrider Press		x				
Outrigger		x				
Overlook Press			x			
Oxford University Press	x		x			
Oxmoor House		. x	Art Books			
Oyez		x				
P & R		x				
Pacific Books		x				
Padre Productions		Before 1994	After 1994			
Pan				Antholo		x

			gies		
Pan Macmillan PTY				x		
Panjandrum			x			
Pantheon Books, Inc.	x					
Para Publishing		x				
Paraclete Press		x				
Paragon House			x			
Parnassus			x			
Pascal Covici		x	Fitfully			
Passport Press		x				
Paternoster		x				
Pathfinder			x			
Pathway Press		x				
Patrice Press		x				
Patrick Stephens Ltd.				x		
Paul A. Struck			x			
Paul Elek		x				
Paul S. Eriksson		x				
Payson & Clarke Ltd.	x	x				
Pegasus Press				x		
Pegasus Publishing			x			
Pelican Publishing		x				
Pelligrini and Cudahy	x					
Pen Rose			x			
Penguin (Australia)				x		
Penmaen Press			x			
Penn Publishing Company	x	x				
Pennsyvania State University Press		x				
Pennyworth Press		x				
Penzler Books			x			
Pequot Press			x			
Peregrine Smith		x				
Pergamon Press Inc.			x			

Perivale Press				x	
Permanent Press		1988-1993	After 1993		
Perry & North		x			
Persea Books			x		
Peter Davies				x	
Peter Halban		x			
Peter Marcan			x		
Peter Owen				x	
Peter Smith	x				
Phaidon Press		x			
Philosophical Library		x			
Philosophical Research			x		
Phoenix Book Shop		x			
Philip Allan & Co.		x			
Philip C. Duschnes		x			
Philosophical Library		x			
Pickering & Inglis LTD		x			
Picton Press		x			
Pictorial Histories		x			
Pineapple Press			After 1985		
Playwrights Canada			x		
Pleiades Books				x	
Plenum		x			
Plough Publishing House		x			
Plympton Press			x		
Pocahontas Press			x		
Poet's Press		x			
Poetry Bookshop		x			
Polygonal		x			
Poolbeg Press		x			
Porpoise Press				x	
Post-Apollo		x			
Potomac Books		x			
Prager				x	
Prentice-Hall		x			
Prentice-Hall		x			

Australia						
Prentice-Hall UK				x		
Preservation Press		x				
Press Porcepic		x				
Pressworks Publishing			x			
Price Milburn				x		
Price/Stern/Sloan			x			
Primavera Press		x				
Princeton University Press	x	x				
Prism Press		x				
Proscenium			x			
Pruett			x			
Puckerbush		x				
Pudding House		x				
Pulp Press		x				
Pulse-Finger Press		x				
Purdue University Press		x				
Purchase Press		x				
Purple Finch Press			x			
Purple Mountain Press			x			
Pushcart Press			x			
Pygmy Forest Press		x				
Pyne Press			x			
Quadrangle		x				
Quail Ridge Press			x			
Quail Street		x				
Quest (Theosophical Society)			x			
Quill & Brush			x			
Quill Driver			x			
Quixote		x				
Quota Press				x		
R.Cobden-Sanderson				x		
R & E		x				
R.H.Russell		x		x		
R.R.Bowker	x	x				

		before 1995	after 1995			
Rabeth Publishing						
Rae D. Henkle Co. Inc.	x					
Ragweed Press		x				
Rainbow Books		x				
Ram			x			
Ramparts Press			x			
Rand McNally & Company	x			x		
Random House Inc.			x			
Ranger International			x			
Ravian Press			x			
Rawson, Wade			x			
Raymond Flatteau			x			
Reader's Digest			Anthol og-ies			x
Real Comet Press			x			
Red Crane			x			
Redbird Press			x			
Reed Books PTY		x				
Reed Publishing LTD				x		
Reference Publications		x				
Regent House			x			
Regnery Gateway		x				
Regular Baptist Press		x				
Reilly & Britton Co.	x	x				
Reilly & Lee Co. Inc.	x	x	After 1937			
Reinhardt Books				x		
Release Press			x			
Renaissance House		x				
Resources for the Future		x				
Reynal and Hitchcock Inc.	x		x			
Rex Collings				x		
Riba		x				

Riccardi Press				x		
Richard G. Badger		x				
Rice University Press			x			
Rich & Cowan			x			
Richard Marek		x				
Richard R. Smith	x	x				
Richard W. Baron Publishing Company Inc.				x		
Richards Press		x				
Rider			x			
Rigby LTD				x		
Rinehart					x	
Rio Grande Press						x
Rising Tide Press			x			
Rivercross			x			
Riverrun				x		
Rizzoli International			x			
Robert Hale		x				
Robert M. McBride & Company			x	x		
Robert R. Knapp		x				
Robert Speller			x			
Robert Welch		x				
Roberts Brothers		x				
Rockbridge			x			
Rockport Press			x			
Rocky Mountain Books		x				
Roland Harvey				x		
Rosendale Press		x				
Rough Guides LTD			x			
Roundwood Press			x			
Routledge				x		
Routledge, Chapman, and Hall				x		

Roulege & Kegan Paul				x		
Roy Publishers Inc.	x					
Royal College of General Practitioners				x		
Royal House			x			
Royal Society		x				
Royal Society of Chemistry		x				
Running Press		x				
Rupert Hart-Davis	x			x		
Russell-Sage		x				
Rutgers University Press	x	x				
S. B. Publications				x		
S. Evelyn Thomas		x				
Saalfield						x
Safari Press			x			
Sagamore Press	x					
Sage Books	x	x				
Sage Publications LTD				x		
Saint Andrews Press				x		
Saint Bede's			x			
St. Botolph		x				
St. Herman of Alaska Brotherhood			x			
St. James Press		x				
St. Martin's Press (Australia)				x		
St. Martin's Press, Inc.		x				
St. Paul's House			x			
Salem House		x				
Saltire House			x	x		
Samuel Curl		x				
Samuel Weiser				x		
San Diego State University		x				

Press					
Sand Dollar		x			
Sandhill Crane Press		x			
Scarlet Press		x			
Scarthin Books				x	
Schoken		x			
SCM Press LTD				x	
Scottish Academic Press		x			
Sea Horse		x			
Search Press				x	
Sears Publishing Company Inc.	x	x			
Seaver			x		
Second Coming		x			
Self-Counsel Press			x		
Selwyn & Blount				x	
Sepher-Hermon Press		x			
Seren Books		x			
Serpent's Tail				x	
Servant Publications		x			
Seven Star			x		
Seymour Lawrence			x		
Shambhala			x		
Sheed & Ward Inc.		x			
Sheffield Academic Press			x		
Sheldon Press				x	
Shengold		x			
Shepheard-Walwyn				x	
Sheridan House Inc.	x	x			
Sherman French & Company		x			
Shire		x			
Shoal Creek		x			
Sidgwick & Jackson				x	

(Australia)						
Sidgwick & Jackson LTD		x				
Sigma Books				x		
Silver Burdett Company		x				
Silver Link				x		
Simon & Schuster	x		x			
Sinclair-Stevenson				x		
Sixteenth Century Journal		x				
Skeffington & Son		x				
Skelton Robinson		x				
Skoob				x		
Sleepy Hollow Restorations			x			
Small Maynard and Company		x				
The Smith			x			
Smith Gryphon				x		
Smith Settle		x				
Society for Promoting Christian Knowledge		x				
Sohnen-Moe			x			
Soho Book Company		x				
Soho Press			x			
Som Publishing		x				
Something Else Press	x	x				
Sono Nis Press		x				
SOS Publications		x				
Southbound Press		x				
Southern Illinois University Press	x	x				
Southern Methodist University Press		x				
Southwest		x				

Press					
Sphere Books		x			
Sphinx			x		
Spindlewood				x	
Spinifex Press				x	
Spoon River			x		
Spring Publications			x		
SR Books				x	
Stackpole Books	x		x		
Stackpole Sons		x			
Stanford University Press	x				
Stanton and Lee		x			
Stanwix House		x			
State Historical Society of Wisconsin	x				
State University Of New York Press		x			
Station Hill			x		
Stream Press		x			
Stein & Day Publishers	x	x			
Stemmer House			x		
Stephen Daye Press	x	x			
Stephen Greene		x		After 1984	
Stephen-Paul			x		
Sterling		x			
Steve Davis			x		
Still Waters Press			x		
Stone and Kimball		x			
Stone Wall Press			x		
Stonehill			x		
Stobart & Sons		x			
Stobart Davies Ltd.		x			
Storm		x			
Stormline Press		x			
Strawberry Hill		x			

Street & Massey				x		
Street and Smith						x
Strether and Swann			x			
Studio Limited		x				
Studio Publications		x				
Sulzberger & Graham		x				
Summit			x			
Sun & Moon Press			x			
Sun Dial						x
Sunflower				x		
Sun Publishing			After 1981			
Sunnyside			x			
Sunset Publishing			x			
Superior Publishing Company	x					
Suttonhouse	x	x	After 1937			
Swallow Press			x			
Swallow Press (Ohio University)		x				
Syracuse University Press	x					
T & A D Poyser				x		
T & T Clark Limited		x				
T. N. Foulis				x		
T. S. Denison		x				
T. Werner Laurie				x		
Tabb House		x				
Tafford			x			
Talbot Press Ltd.	x					
Talisman House		x				
Talon Books		x	After 1994			
Tamaroack Books		x				
Tamarack			x			

Press						
Tandem Press (New Zealand)				x		
Tandem Press (U. S.)		x				
Taplinger Publishing Co. Inc.			x			
Tatsch		x				
Taunton Press			x			
Temple University Press		x				
Texas A & M University Press			x			
Texas Christian University Press		x				
Texas Monthly Press			x			
Texas Tech University Press			x			
Texas Western Press		x				
Thames and Hudson Inc.				x		
Thames and Hudson Ltd.		x				
Thames and Hudson Pty.		x				
Theater Arts			x			
Theosophical Publishing House (Wheaton)			x			
Theosophical University Press			x			
Thistledown Press		x				
Thomas Jefferson University		x				
Thomas Nelson & Sons				x		
Thomas Seltzer		x				
Thomas Telford				x		
Thomas Y. Crowell	x	After19				

		26				
Thorndike Press						x
Thornton Butterworth				x		
Thorson's				x		
Thunder's Mouth		before 1993	after 1993			
Tia Chucha		x				
Ticknor & Fields	x	x				
Ticknor and Company	x	x				
Tilbury House			x			
Times Books			x			
Tolley Publishing				x		
TOR			x			
Tory Corner Editions			x			
Tower						x
Town House and Country House				x		
Trail's End Publishing Inc.			x			
Transaction Books		x				
Transatlantic Arts			x			
Transportation Trails				x		
Treehaus			x			
Trend House		x				
Triangle						x
Trident Press	x	x				
Trigon Press				x		
Triumph			x			
Troubador			x			
Trout Creek		x				
TSG		x				
Tundra Books of Montreal		x				
Tundra Books of Northern New York		x				
Turner Co.		x				
Turner Publishing		x				
Turnstone				x		
Turtle Island		x				
Turton &		x				

Armstrong PTY					
Twayne Publishers Inc.	x	x			
Twentieth Century Fund		x			
Twenty-Third Publications		x			
Two Bytes			x		
UCL Press				x	
Underwood-Miller			x		
Unicorn Press				x	
Universe Books		x			
University Books		x			
University Classics		x			
University College of Cape Breton Press				x	
University of Alabama Press	x				
University of Alaska Press			x		
University of Arizona Press	x	x			
University of Arkansas Press		x			
University of British Columbia Press		x			
University of Calgary Press		x			
University of California Press	x	x			
University of Chicago Press	x	x			
University of Colorado Press	x				
University of Georgia Press		x			
University of Hull Press		x			
University of Illinois Press	x				
University of Iowa Press		Before 1985	After 1985		
University of		x			

Kansas Museum of Natural History					
University of Kentucky Press	x				
University of Massachusetts Press		x			
University of Miami Press	x				
University of Michigan Press	x				
University of Minnesota Press	x				
University of Missouri Press		x			
University of Montana Linguistics Laboratory				x	
University of Nebraska Press	x				
University of New Mexico Press			x		
University of New South Wales		x			
University of North Carolina Press	x	x			
University of Oklahoma Press			x		
University Of Otago Press				x	
University of Pennsylvania Press	x	x			
University of Pittsburgh Press	x				
University of Queensland Press		x			
University of Rochester Press		x			
University of South Carolina Press			x		
University of	x		x		

Tennessee Press					
University of Texas Press	x				
University of Utah Press		x			
University of Wales Press		x			
University of Washington Press	x				
University of Western Australia Press				x	
University of Wisconsin Press	Before 1970		After 1970		
University Press of America		x			
University Press of Colorado		x			
University Press of Florida		x			
University Press of Hawaii		x			
University Press of Kansas		x			
University Press of Mississippi		x			
University Press of New England		x			
University Press of Virginia		x			
University Presses of Florida		x			
University Society		x			
Unwin, Hyman, Inc.		x			
Unwin, Hyman Limited				x	
Urban Institute			x		
Ure Smith			x	x	
Urizen Books		x			

U. S. Games Systems			x			
Van Nostrand Reinhold		x				
Van Petten		x				
Vandamere		x				
Vanguard Press	x					
Vedanta		x				
Veloce				x		
Vestal Press		x				
Victor Gollancz		x				
Victoria University Press				x		
Viet Nam Generation		x				
Viking Penguin		x				
Viking UK			x			
Viking Press		x		x		
Villard			x			
Virago Press				x		
Virgin				x		
Vision Books			x			
Vixen		x				
W.A.Wilde Company	x	x				
W. D. Hoard		x				
W. H. Freeman		x				
W. Heffer & Sons		x				
W. Heinemann				x		
W. H. & O.			x			
Wm. B. Eerdmans		x				
W & R Chambers			x			
W. W. Norton			Before 1976			
Wadsworth Publishing		x				
Wake-Brook House			x			
Walker and Co.				x		
Walter McVitty				x		
Walter Neale		x				
Ward Lock				x		
Warren H.		x				

Green						
Wartburg Press		x				
Washington Researchers			x			
Washington State University Press			x			
Water Row Press			x			
Waterfront			x			
Watermark Press		x				
Watson-Guptill		x	x			
Way and Williams		x				
Wayne State University Press		x				
Weatherhill			x			
Webb Publishing			x			
Webb Research		x				
Weidenfeld & Nicholson				x		
Westcott Cove		x				
Wesleyan University Press			x			
West Coast Poetry Review		x				
Western Producer Prarie Books		x				
Western Reserve University	x					
Westernlore	x	x				
Westland		x				
Westminster Press		After 1977				
Westminster/John Knox			x			
Westview		x				
Weybright and Talley Inc.	x					
Wheat Forders				x		
White Cockade		x				
White Pine		x				
Whitehorse Press		x				

Whitney Library of Design				x	
Whitson			x		
Whittlesey House	x				
Widescope International PTY				x	
Wilde & Johnson					x
Wilderness Press		x			
Wilfred Funk		x			
Willet, Clarke and Company	x	x			
William Blackwood & Sons		x			
William Carey Library		x			
William Collins PTY				x	
William Collins & Son		x			
William Edward Rudge		x			
William-Fredrick Press	x				
William Godwin	x				
William Heinemann		Before 1920		After 1920	
William Kimber				x	
William L. Bauhan		x			
William Morrow & Co. Inc.		After 1976	Before 1976		
William Penn Publishing Company	x				
William R. Scott				x	
William Sloane Associates Inc.			x		
Williams & Northgate				x	
Williams & Wilkins		x			
Wilfred Funk			x		
Winchester		x			

Press					
Windrush Press				x	
Windswept House		x			
Windward House		x			
Windward Publishing		x			
Wingbow Press		Before 1981	After 1981		
Winslow				x	
Winston-Derek		x			
Wisconsin House			x		
Wishart		After 1935		Before 1935	
Witherby			x		
Wolfhound Press		x			
Woman's Press			x		
Wood Lake		x			
Woodbridge Press		x			
World Bank			x		
World Leisure		x			
World Publishing Company			x		
World Resources		x			
World Scientific		x			
Yachting		x			
Yale Center for British Art		x			
Yale University Press	x			x	
Yankee			x		
Ye Galleon					x
Yellow Hook			x		
Zephyr Press			x		
Zephyrus Press			x		
Zero Press			x		
Ziff-Davis Limited				x	
Ziff-Davis Publishing Company	x	x			
Ziggurat Press		x			
Zoland Books			x		

Zondervan		x				

American & British Publishers Using Unique or Semi-unique Methods

D.Appleton & Co. Appleton-Century Crofts*- The print run is at the end of the text, (1) being a First Edition.

Arcadia House - No date on Title page "1" on the verso.

Arkham House- Carried a colophon page with edition noted at the end of the text.

Black Sparrow - Edition and Printing noted on colophon page in the rear and the title page printed in color.

Bruce Publishing (St. Paul, MN) - The printing is indicated in the lower left corner of the last page.

Carrick & Evans Inc.- First Editions have an "A" on the verso.

Cokesbury Press- First Editions have a "C" at the foot of the verso.

Coward-McCann - To 1936 put a colophon on verso, a colophon with a torch signified a first edition

Thomas Y. Crowell Company Inc.- The First Edition has a "1" at the foot of the verso.

Jonathon David - A number "1" above the date on the verso indicates a first edition.

Stanley Gibbons- The Edition number is carried on the title page.

Golden Cockerell- A limited edition publisher, exceptions to exclusive first editions in their line (reprints) are: Adam & Eve & Pinch Me (1921), Rummy (1932), and Tapster's Tapestry (1938) by A. E. Coppard; Tersichore & Other Poems (1921) bt H.T.Wade-Gery; The Puppet Show (1922) by Matin Armstrong; Consequences (1932) and Anthology; The Hansom Cab and the Pigeons (1935) by L. A. G. Strong; The Epicure's Anthology (1936) edited by Nancy Quennell; The Tale of the Golden Cockerell (1936) by A. S. Pushkin; Chanticleer (1936) a Bibliography; Ana the Runner (1937) by Patrick Miller; Here's Flowers (1937) An Anthology Edited by Joan Ritter; Mr. Chambers and Persephone (1937), and The Lady from Yesterday (1939) by Christopher Whitfield; Goat Green (1937) by T. F. Pwys; The White Llama (1938) being the La Venganza del Condor of V. G. Calderon; Brief Candles (1938) by Lawrence Binyon; and The Wisdom of the Cymry (1939) by Winifred Faraday.

Grune & Stratton- "A" on the last page of the index indicates a first printing.

Harcourt Brace etc.*- No date on Title page "1" on the verso. Also "First Edition" over a line of letters beginning with B.

Harper etc.- Uses all methods except 5. From 1912 to 1971 used a number code for Month and Year, month starting with A-January through M (excepting J) December followed by the year alphabetically beginning with M-1912, and returning to A in 1926, and 1951. Code corresponding to copyright date is a First. Thusly:

A-Jan	G-Jul
B-Feb	H-Aug
C-Mar	I-Sep
D-Apr	K-Oct
E-May	L-Nov
F-Jun	M-Dec

M-1912	A-1926	P-1940
N-1913	B-1927	Q-1941
O-1914	C-1928	R-1942
P-1915	D-1929	S-1943
Q-1916	E-1930	T-1944
R-1917	F-1931	U-1945
S-1918	G-1932	V-1946
T-1919	H-1933	W-1947
U-1920	I-1934	X-1948
V-1921	K-1935	Y-1949
W-1922	L-1936	
X-1923	M-1937	
Y-1924	N-1938	
Z-1925	O-1939	

Herald Press- Before 1993 carried the publication date below the publisher's imprint on the title page on
first editions only.
IGI Publications- A number "1" next to the last page number signifies a first edition.
Wayne L. McNaughton- Three numbers seperated by . as 1.1.1. The first is the stock number, second, edition, third, print run
Mycroft & Moran- Carried a colophon page with edition noted at the end of the text.
Permanent Press- Carried a colophon page with edition noted at the end of the text.
Random House- "First Edition" stated over a number line beginning at 2 (changed to standard line beginning at 1 during 2004).
Charles Scribner's Sons*- Between 1929 and 1973 an "A" on the verso designated a First. A colophon accompanying the A was fitfully used at the foot of the verso.
Martin Secker- Bibliographic history on the verso.
Martin Secker & Warburg- Bibliographic history on the verso.
Sheed & Ward LTD- Bibliographic history on the verso.
Frederick Warne & Co. Inc.- A number 1 at the foot of the verso is a First.
Franklin Watts Inc.*- A number 1 at the foot of the verso is a First.

Printers' Codes

A printer's code may be a simple line of numbers or letters on the verso, or may be more complicated giving such facts as the year, or month of publication.

Examples of a first printing:

        1 2 3 4 5 6 7 8 9 10
        10 9 8 7 6 5 4 3 2 1

A B C D
    a b c d e f g

Subsequent printings remove the runs completed, for example:
3 4 5 6 7 8 9 10 is a third printing.
Later printings may carry a single number or a series, the lowest being the current print run for example:

Both "25 26 27" and "25" indicate the twenty-fifth printing.
A more complicated code might read

        1 2 3 4 5 6   91 92 93 94 95

which would be a first printing in the year 1991, you would then check the copyright date to verify a first edition (ie: the copyright date would have to be 1991).
The print code indicates a print run. In and of itself it does not always guarentee a first edition, only a first printing which may be a second, or special edition of the work. However, on most books originally published with ISBN numbers, the print code verification can be taken as indicating a first edition, if no conflicting evidence is present.

Cautions

There are many factors in looking for first editions. Publishers are a bit lax in designating them and often use the same plates without variation or with minor variations when they reprint, and children's books often do not follow the conventions. For more expensive and collectible books, as well as the books of known and collectible authors, the variations are known and noted in bibliographies, the standard in American books being the Bibliography of American Literature (abbreviated BAL). There are, however, a few obvious factors.

Book Club Editions

There are certain "give-aways" to book club Editions. First, check the dust jacket, if one is present. Is it priced? If not, be suspicious. Book of the Month Club stamps the back cover on the lower right with some geometric symbol, either printed on the cloth or indented (debossed). Some BOMC editions carry a code (JK5H, for example) near the bottom of the last few pages. Does it feel light? Book clubs use thinner paper. Does it have a headband (small pieces of cloth inside the top, bottom or along the spine)? If not, be suspicious.

Reprint Publishers

Some publishers specialize in reprinting . So, while a book may look like a first edition given any standard of marking, it is a reprint. Grosset and Dunlap, J.Walter Black, A.L.Burt are all reprint publishers and rarely produced original works.

Pseudonyms

There are numerous reasons for an author using a pseudonym. None of which make a great deal of sense. Amandine-Aurore-Lucile Dupin parading around Paris in men's clothes, smoking cigars and calling herself George might have made some point if she didn't have rather public affairs with Polish composers, for example. And don't ask about Aleister (Edward Alexander) Crowley. I'm sorry I started with him and I have no idea why he has more pseudonyms than most writers have books. Still in all it is a very good idea for a book collector to check and see if their favorite author isn't trying to fool them by writing as someone else, or maybe becoming famous as someone else and then trying to slip one past everyone using their real name.

A.	**Matthew Arnold**
A, Dr.	**Isaac Asimov**
Aallyn, Alysse	**Melissa Clarke**
Aaron, Sidney	**Paddy Chayefsky**
Abbott, Anthony	**(Charles) Fulton Oursler**
Abdullah, Achmed	**Alexander Romanoff**
Abramowitz, Joseph	*Joey Adams*
Acre, Stephen	**Frank Gruber**
Acton, R.	**Emily Bronte**
Adams, Andy	**Walter B. Gibson**
Adams, Joey	**Abramowitz, Joseph**
Adams, Samuel Hopkins	*Warner Fabian*
Adams, William Taylor	*Warren T. Ashton*
	Oliver Optic
Aadoff, Virginia Esther Hamilton	*Virginia Hamilton*
A.E.	**George William Russell**
Aghill, Gordon	**Randall Garrett & Robert Silverberg**
Aiken, Conrad	*Samuel Jeake*
Ainslie, Arthur	**Arthur Welesley Pain**
Ainsworth, Harriet	**Elizabeth Cadell**
Akers, Alan Burt	**Kenneth Bulmer**
Akers, Floyd	**L. Frank Baum**
Alastor	**Edward Alexander Crowley**
Alastor le Demon du Solitude	**Edward Alexander Crowley**
Albano, Peter	*Andrea Robbins*
Albert, Marvin H.	*Al Conroy*
	Ian McAllister
	Nick Quarry
	Anthony (Tony) Rome
Alcott, Louisa May	*A.M. Barnard*
Alden, Isabella MacDonald	*Pansy*
Aldington, Hilda Doolittle	**Hilda Doolittle**
Aldiss, Brian W.	*C.C. Shackleton*
Aleichem, Sholem	**Sholem Yakov Rabinowitz**
Alekseyev, Constantin Sergeyevich	*Constantin Stanislavsky*
Alexander, Bruce	*Bruce Cook*
Alexander, Ed	**Edward Emshmiller**
Alger, Horatio	Arthur Lee Putnam
	Julian Starr

Allan, John B.	**Donald Westlake**
Allen, Charles Grant Blairfindie	*Grant Allen*
	Cecil Power
	Olive Pratt Rayne
	Joseph Warborough
	Martin Leach Warborough
Allen, Grant	**Charles Grant Blairfindie Allen**
Allen, Hervey	**William Hervey Allen Jr.**
Allen, Steve	*William Allen Stevens*
	William Christopher Stevens
Allen, William Hervey, Jr.	*Hervey Allen*
	Hardly Alum
Allen, Woody	**Allen Stewart Konigsberg**
Allingham, Margery Louise	*Margery Allingham Carter*
	Maxwell March
	Margery Allingham Youngman-Carter
Allison, Clay	**Henry John Keevil**
Allison, Clyde	**William Knowles**
Almquist, John	*Victor W. Appleton II*
Alum, Hardly	**William Hervey Allen Jr.**
Alzee, Grendon	**Arthur Leo Zagat**
Ambler, Eric	*Eliot Reed*
Amery, Francis	**Brian Stableford**
Ames, Clyde	**William Knowles**
Amis, Kingsley	*Robert Markham*
	William Tanner
Amory, Guy	**Ray Bradbury**
Andersen, Hans Christian	*Christian Walter Killiam*
Anderson, David	**Raymond F. Jones**
Anderson, Maxwell	*John Nairne Michaelson*
Anderson, Poul	*A.A. Craig*
	Michael Karageorge
	Winston P. Sanders
Anderson, Roberta	*Fern Michaels*
Andrews, Cicily Isabel Fairfield	*Rebecca West*
Andrews, Cleo Virginia	*V.C. Andrews*
Andrews, Elton V.	**Fred Pohl**
Andrews, Felicia	**Charles L. Grant**
Andrews, V.C.	**Cleo Virginia Andrews and Andrew Neiderman**
Andrezel, Pierre	**Karen Christence Blixen-Finecke**
Andrus, L.R.	*Lee Andre*
Angelique, Pierre	**Georges Bataille**
Ankh-af-na-Khonsu	**Edward Alexander Crowley**
Anmar, Frank	**William F. Nolan**
Ansle, Dorothy Phoebe	*Laura Conway*
	Hebe Elsna
	Vicky Lancaster
	Lyndon Snow
Anstey, F.	**Thomas Anstey Guthrie**
Anthony, Evelyn	**Evelyn Ward-Thomas**
Anthony, John	**John Ciardi** and **John S. Littel**
Ant(h)ony, Peter	**Anthony (Joshua) Shaffer** and **Peter Levin Shaffer**
Anthony, Piers	**Piers Anthony Dillingham Jacob**
Antoine, Eduoard Charles	*Emile Zola*
Antonius, Brother	**William Everson**
Apollinaire, Guillaume	**Wilhelm de Kostrowitski**
Appel, H.M.	**Wayne Rogers**
Appleton, Laurence	**H(oward) P(hillips) Lovecraft**
Appleton, Victor	**Howard R. Garis**
	Edward L. Stratemeyer
Appleton, Victor W., II	**Harriet S. Adams**

	John Almquist
	Neil Barrett
	Vincent Buranelli
	Sharman DiVono
	William Dougherty
	Debra Doyle
	Steven Grant
	James Duncan Lawrence
	F. Gwynplaine MacIntrye
	James D. Macdonald
	Bill McCay
	Bridget McKenna
	Richard McKenna
	Mike McQuay
	Thomas Mulvey
	William Rotsler
	Richard Sklar
	Robert E. Vardeman
Archer, Catherine	**Catherine J. Archibald**
Archer, Frank	**Richard O'Connor**
Archer, Lee	**Harlan Ellison**
Archer, Ron	D. Van Arnam *and* **Theodore Edward White**
Archibald, Catherine J.	*Catherine Archer*
Ard, William	*Ben Kerr*
	Mike Moran
	Jonas Ward
	Thomas Wills
Ariel	**Edward Alexander Crowley**
Arion	**G(ilbert) K(eith) Chesterton**
Arlen, Michael	**Dikran Kuyamjian**
Arno, Peter	**Curtis Arnoux Peters**
Arnold, Matthew	*A.*
Arnow, Harriette	**Harriet Simpson**
Aronin, Ben	**Edna Herron**
Arouet, François Marie	*Catherine Vadé*
	Guillaume Vadé
	Voltaire
Arp, Bill	**Charles H. Smith**
Asch, Shalom	*Rufus Learsi*
Ashcroft, Laura	**Janice Carlson**
Ashdown, Clifford	R. Austin Freeman and J. J. Pitcairn
Ashe, Gordon	**John Creasey**
Ashton, Winifred	*Clemence Dane*
Asimov, Isaac	*Dr. A*
	George E. Dale
	The Good Doctor
	Paul French
	H.B. Ogden
A Square	**Edwin A. Abbott**
Asquith, Lady Cynthia	**Mary Evelyn Charteris**
Aston, Sharon	**Helen Van Slyke**
Atherton, Gertrude Franklin	*Gertrude Franklin Horn*
	Frank Lin
Auchincloss, Louis	*Andrew Lee*
Audemars, Pierre	*Peter Hodemart*
August, John	**Bernard Augustine De Voto**
Aumont, Gerard	**Edward Alexander Crowley**
Aunt Hattie	**Harriett Newell Baker**
Austin, Brett	**Lee Floren**
Austin, Mary H.	*Gordon Stairs*
Authoress, The	**Edward Alexander Crowley**

Axton, David	**Dean R. Koontz**
B	**A. C. Benson**
B., C.	**Charlotte Brontë**
B., H.	**Joseph Pierre Hilaire Belloc**
B., J.K.	**John Kendrick Bangs**
Bachman, Richard	**Stephen King**
Baker, Ray Stannard	*David Grayson*
Baker, Harriet Newell	*Aunt Hattie*
Ballard, K.G.	**Holly Roth**
Bancroft, Laura	**L. Frank Baum**
Bandoff, Hope	**Thomas Anstey Guthrie**
Bangs, John Kendrick	*J.K.B.*
	T. Carlyle Smith
	Anne Warrington Witherup
Banks, Edward	**Ray Bradbury**
Baphomet, X',	**Edward Alexander Crowley**
Baraka, Imamu Amiri	**Leroi Jones**
Bardwell, Harrison	**Edith Janice Craine**
Barclay, Bill	**Michael Moorcock**
Barclay, Gabriel	**C(yril) M. Kornbluth**
Barclay, William Ewert	**Michael Moorcock**
Barham, Richard	*Thomas Ingoldsby*
Barnard, A.M.	**Louisa May Alcott**
Barnes, Djuna	*Lydia Steptoe*
Barr, Robert	*Luke Sharp*
Barrett, Neil, Jr.	*Victor W. Appleton II*
Barretton, Grandal	**Randall Garrett**
Barrington, E.	**L(ily) Adams Beck**
Barrington, Michael	**Michael Moorcock**
Barry, Jonathan	**Whitley Strieber**
Barry, Mike	**Barry N(orman) Malzberg**
Barshuck, Grego	**Hugo Gernsback**
Barstow, Mrs. Montague	*Baroness Orczy*
	Emma Magdalena Rosalia Maria Josefa Barbara Orczy
Barton, Eustace Robert	*Robert Eustace*
	Eustace Rawlins
Bataille, Georges	*Pierre Angelique*
Baum, L(yman) Frank	*Floyd Akers*
	Laura Bancroft
	John Estes Cook
	John Estes Cooke
	Hugh Fitzgerald
	Suzanne Metcalf
	Schuyler Stanton
	Schuyler Staunton
	Edith Van Dyne
Bax, Roger	**Paul Winterton**
Baxter, George Owen	**Frederick Schiller Faust**
Bean, Norman	**Edgar Rice Burroughs**
Beast, The 666	**Edward Alexander Crowley**
Beck, Eliza Louisa Moresby	**L(ily) Adams Beck**
Beck, L(ily) Adams	*E. Barrington*
	Eliza Louisa Moresby Beck
	L(ouis) Moresby
Beecher, Harriet (Elizabeth)	*Christopher Crowfield*
,	*Harriet Beecher Stowe*
Behle-Stendahl, Henry	**Marie-Henri Beyle**
Beldone, Cheech	**Harlan Ellison**
Beldone, Phil	**Harlan Ellison**
Bell, Acton	**Anne Brontë**
Bell, Alexander Graham	*H.A. Largelamb*

Bell, Currer	**Charlotte Brontë**
Bell, Ellis	**Emily (Jane) Brontë**
Bell, Eric Temple	*J.T.*
	John Taine
Bellairs, George	**Harold Blundell**
Bellin, Edward J.	**C(yril) M. Kornbluth** and **Henry Kuttner**
Belloc, Joseph Pierre Hilaire	*H.B.*
Benchley, Robert	*Guy Fawkes*
Bendick, Francis	**Edward Alexander Crowley**
Bennett, Arnold	*Jacob Tonson Gwendolyn*
Benson, A(rthur) C(hristopher)	*B. Christopher Carr*
Berkeley, Anthony	**A(nthony) B(erkeley) Cox**
Berryman, John	*Walter Bupp*
	John Allyn Smith
Bester, Alfred	*John Lennox*
	Sonny Powell
Bethlen, T.D.	**Robert Silverberg**
Betjeman, (Sir) John	*Richard M. Farren*
Bey, Pilaff	**Norman Douglas**
Beyle, Marie-Henri	*Henry Behle-Stendahl*
	Stendahl
	Baron de Stendahl
Beynon, John	**John Wyndham Parkes Lucas Beynon Harris**
Bierce, Ambrose (Gwinnett)	*Dod Grile*
	William Herman
	J. Milton Sloluck
Bigby, Cantell A.	**George W. Peck**
Biglow, Hosea	**James Russell Lowell**
Billings, Josh	**Henry Wheeler Shaw**
Binder, Eando	**Earl Andrew Binder** and **Otto O(scar) Binder**
Binder, Earl Andrew	*Eando Binder*
	Jack Binder
	John Coleridge
	Gordon A. Giles
	Dean D. O'Brien
Binder, Jack	**Earl Andrew Binder** and **Otto O(scar) Binder**
Binder, Otto O(scar)	*Eando Binder*
	Jack Binder
	John Coleridge
	Will Garth
	Gordon A. Giles
	Dean D. O'Brien
Bird, C(ordwainer)	**Harlan Ellison**
Bird, Cordwainer	**Philip José Farmer**
Birdwell, Cleo	**Don DeLillo**
Bishop, Alison	*Alison Lurie*
Bishop, George Archibald	**Edward Alexander Crowley**
Black, Ishi	**Walter B(rown) Gibson**
Blair, Eric Arthur	*George Orwell*
Blake, Andrew	**Randall Garrett** and **Larry M(ark) Harris**
Blake, Nicholas	**C(ecil) D(ay) Lewis**
Blake, Patrick	**Clive Egleton**
Bland, E(dith Nesbit) ·	*Fabian Bland*
	E. Nesbit
Bland, Fabian	**E(dith Nesbit) Bland**
Blight, Rose	**Germaine Greer**
Blish, James (Benjamin)	*William Atheling Jr.*
	Donald Laverty
	Marcus Lyons
	John MacDougal
	Arthur Merlyn

Bliss, Reginald	**H(erbert) G(eorge) Wells**
Blixen-Finecke, Karen Christence	*Pierre Andrezel*
	Isak Dinesen
	Osceola
Bloch, Robert (Albert)	*Tarleton Fiske*
	Will Folke
	Nathan Hindin
	E.K. Jarvis
	Wilson Kane
	Jim Kjelgaard
	Sherry Malone
	John Sheldon
	Collier Young
Block, Lawrence	*Chip Harrison*
	Paul Kavanagh
Blundell, Harold	*George Bellairs*
Blutig, Eduard	**Edward (St. John) Gorey**
Bobette	**Georges Simenon**
Boehm, Herb	**John (Herbert) Varley**
Bogart, William Henry	*Kenneth Robeson*
	Sentinel
Boissevain, Edna St. Vincent Millay	**Edna St. Vincent Millay**
Bok, Hannes	**Wayne Woodard**
Boleskine, Lord	**Edward Alexander Crowley**
Bond, Nelson S(lade)	*George Danzell*
	Hubert Mavity
Bonner, Terry Nelson	**Chelsea Quinn Yarbro**
Borges, Jorge Luís	*H(onorio) Bustos Domecq*
	B. Suárez Lynch
Boston, Charles K.	**Frank Gruber**
Boucher, Anthony	**William Anthony Parker White**
Bova, Ben	*Oxford Williams*
Box, Edgar	**Eugene Luther Gore Vidal Jr.**
Boyd, Nancy	**Edna St. Vincent Millay**
Boz	**Charles Dickens**
Brackett, Leigh (Douglass)	*George Sanders*
	Eric John Stark
Bradbury, E(dward) P.	**Michael (John) Moorcock**
Bradbury, Ray(mond Douglas)	*Guy Amory*
	D.R. Banat
	Edward Banks
	Anthony Corvais
	Cecil Clairbourne Cunningham
	E. Cunningham
	Leonard Douglas
	Brian Eldred
	William Elliott
	Hollerbochen
	Omega
	Ron Reynolds
	Doug Rogers
	Douglas Spaulding
	Leonard Spaulding
	Brett Sterling
	D. Lerium Tremaine
Bradley, Marion Zimmer	*Lee Chapman*
	John Dexter
	Miriam Gardner
	Valerie Graves
	Morgan Ives
	Brian Morley

	Dee O'Brien
	John Jay Wells
Bradshaw, William	*Christopher Isherwood*
Bramah, Ernest	**Ernest Bramah Smith**
Branch, Stephen	**Stefan Zweig**
Brand, Max	**Frederick Schiller Faust**
Bridgeport, Robert	**Robert Crichton**
Bridges, Robert	*Droch*
Brinburning, Algernon Robert Charles	**Edward Alexander Crowley**
Brontë, Anne	*Acton Bell*
	Lady Geralda
	Olivia Vernon
	Alexandria Zenobia
Brontë, Charlotte	*C.B.*
	Currer Bell
	Marquis of Douro
	Genius
	Lord Charles Wellesley
Brontë, Emily (Jane)	*R. Acton*
	Ellis Bell
Brown, Douglas	**Walter B(rown) Gibson**
Brown, Morna Doris (MacTaggart)	*E.X. Ferrars*
	Elizabeth Ferrars
Brulls, Christian	**Georges Simenon**
Brune, Madame Bock	**Edward Alexander Crowley**
Brunner, John (Kilian Houston)	*Kilian Houston Brunner*
	Kilian Houston
	Gill Hunt
	Wolfgang Kurtz
	John Loxmith
	Trevor Staines
	Keith Woodcott
Brunner, Kilian Houston	**John (Kilian Houston) Brunner**
Buchanan, Jack	**Joe R. Lansdale**
Buck, Pearl S(ydenstricker)	*John Sedges*
	Pearl Sydenstricker Buck Walsh
Budrys, Algirdas Jonas	*Algis Budrys*
	David C. Hodgkins
	Ivan Janvier
	Paul Janvier
	Robert Marner
	Frank Mason
	Jeffries Oldmann
	Alger Rome
	William Scarff
	John A. Sentry
	Albert Stroud
	Harold Van Dall
Budrys, Algis	**Algirdas Jonas Budrys**
Bupp, Walter	**John Berryman**
	Randall Garrett
Buranelli, Vincent	*Victor W. Appleton II*
Burke, Ralph	**Randall Garrett** and **Robert Silverberg**
Burke, Robert	**Robert Silverberg**
Burns, Tex	**Louis Dearborn LaMoore**
Burroughs, Edgar Rice	*Norman Bean*
	Craig Shaw Gardner
	John Tyler McCulloch
	John Tyler McCullough
Burroughs, William S.	*Willy (William) Lee*
C., A.E.	**Edward Alexander Crowley**

C., E.A.	**Edward Alexander Crowley**
C., G.K.	**G(ilbert) K(eith) Chesterton**
C., H.	**Edward Alexander Crowley**
C., J.	**Edward Alexander Crowley**
Cabell, Branch	**James Branch Cabell**
Cabell, James Branch	*Branch Cabell*
	Henry Lee Jefferson
	Berwell Washington
Cain	**Edward Alexander Crowley**
Caligula	**Edward Alexander Crowley**
Campbell, (John) Ramsey	*Carl Dreadstone*
	Jay Ramsay
	Errol Undercliffe
Campbell, John W., Jr.	**John Wood Campbell**
Campbell, John Wood	*John W. Campbell Jr.*
	Arthur McCann
	Don A. Stuart
	Karl Van Campen
Campen, Karl Van	**John Wood Campbell, Jr.**
Candlestick	**Edward Alexander Crowley**
Canning, Victor	*Alan Gould*
Cannon, Curt	**Salvatore A. Lombino**
Cantab	**Edward Alexander Crowley**
Capp, Al	**Alfred G(erard) Caplin**
Card, Orson Scott	Dinah Kirkham
	Noam D. Pellume
	Bryon Walley
Carey, The Reverend P.D.	**Edward Alexander Crowley**
Carr, D.	**Edward Alexander Crowley**
Carr, H.D.	**Edward Alexander Crowley**
Carr, John Dickson	*Carter Dickenson*
	Carr Dickson
	Carter Dickson
	Roger Fairbairn
	Torquemada
Carrington, Hereward	*Nancy Fodor*
	Hubert Lavington
Carter, Margery Allingham	**Margery Louise Allingham**
Cartmill, Cleve	*Michael Corbin*
	George Sanders
Cary, Arthur Joyce Lunel	*Joyce Cary*
Cary, Joyce	**Arthur Joyce Lunel Cary**
Casey, John	**Sean O'Casey**
Casseres, Benjamin De	**Clark Ashton Smith**
Casside, John	**Sean O'Casey**
Cave, Hugh B.	*Justin Case*
	Geoffrey Vace
Cerebellum	**Edward Alexander Crowley**
C.G.R.	**Christine G. Rossetti**
Chaney, John Griffith	*Jack London*
Chapin, Paul	**Philip José Farmer**
Chapman, Lee	**Marion Zimmer Bradley**
Chapman, Walter	**Robert Silverberg**
Charles, J.K.	**Georges Simenon**
Charles, Steven	**Charles L(ewis) Grant**
Charteris, Leslie	**Leslie C(harles) B(owyer) Yin**
Charteris, Mary Evelyn	*Lady Cynthia Asquith*
Chatrian, Alexandre	*Erckmann-Chatrian*
Chase, Josephine	*Jessie Graham Flower*
Chaucer, Daniel	**Ford Madox Hueffer**
Chayefsky, Paddy	*Sidney Aaron*

Chesbro, George C.	*David Cross*
Chesney, Weatherby	**C(harles) J(ohn) Cutcliffe (Wright) Hyne**
Chester, Miss Di	**Dorothy L(eigh) Sayers**
Chesterton, G(ilbert) K(eith)	*Arion*
	G.K.C.
Chris, Leonard	**Dean (Ray) Koontz**
Mary Clarissa Miller Mallowan	*Agatha Christie*
	Agatha Christie Mallowan
	Mary Westmacott
Christilian, J.D.	*Michael Barone*
	Al Conroy
	Ian MacAlister
	Nick Quarry
	Anthony (Tony) Rome
Churton, Henry	**Albion W(inegar) Tourgée**
Ciardi, John	*John Anthony*
Clark, Curt	**D(onald) E(dwin) Westlake**
Clarke, Arthur C(harles)	*E.G. O'Brien*
	Charles Willis
Clemens, Samuel Langhorne	*Mark Twain*
Clement, Hal	**Harry Clement Stubbs**
Cleri, Mario	**Mario Puzo**
Clerk, N.W.	**C(live) S(taples) Lewis**
C.M. of the Vigilantes	**Edward Alexander Crowley**
Cody, John	**Ed(ward) Earl Repp**
Coe, Tucker	**D(onald) E(dwin) Westlake**
Coeli, Sir Meduim	**Edward Alexander Crowley**
Coffey, Brian	**Dean (Ray) Koontz**
Coffin, Peter	**Jonathan (Wyatt) Latimer**
Cole, Burt	**Thomas Dixon**
Coleman, Emmett	**Ishmael Reed**
Coles, Cyril H(enry)	*Manning Coles*
	Francis Gaite
Coles, Manning	**Cyril H(enry) Coles and Adelaide F(rancis) O(ke) Manning**
Colette	**Sidonie-Gabrielle Colette**
Colette, Sidonie-Gabrielle	*Colette*
	Mme Maurice Goudeket
	Mme Henri de Jouvenal
Collins, Hunt	**Salvatore A. Lombino**
Collinson, Peter	**Samuel Dashiell Hammett**
Colvin, James	**Michael (John) Moorcock**
Connor, Ralph	**Charles William Gordon**
Conrad, Joseph	**Jósef Teodor Konrad Korzeniowski**
Constant, Alphonse L.	*Eliphas Levi*
Conway, Graham	**Donald A(llen) Wollheim**
Cook, John Estes	**L(yman) Frank Baum**
Cooke, Arth	**C(yril) M. Kornbluth and Robert (Augustine) W(ard) Lowndes**
Cooke, John Estes	**L(yman) Frank Baum**
Cooke, Margaret	**John Creasey**
Cooke, M.E.	**John Creasey**
Cooper, Henry St. John	**John Creasey**
Cooper, James Fenimore	*Jane Morgan*
Copper, Basil	*Lee Falk*
Corbin, Michael	**Cleve Cartmill**
Corelli, Marie	**Mary MacKay**
Cornwell, David John Moore	*John LeCarré*
Cor Scorpionis	**Edward Alexander Crowley**
Corvais, Anthony	**Ray(mond Douglas) Bradbury**
Corvo, Baron (Frederick)	**Frederick William Rolfe**
Corwin, Cecil	**C(yril) M. Kornbluth**
Costa, Henry De	**Frederik Pohl**

Costler, A.	**Arthur Koestler**
Counselman, Mary Elizabeth	*Charles DuBois*
	Sanders McCrorey
	John Starr
Courtney, Robert	**Harlan (Jay) Ellison** and **C(harles) Daly King**
Coward, (Sir) Noel (Pierce)	*Hernia Whittlebot*
Cox, A(nthony) B(erkeley)	*Anthony Berkeley*
	Frances Iles
	A. Monmouth Platts
Craig, James	**Roy. J. Snell**
Craig, Webster	**Eric F(rank) Russell**
Craine, Edith Janice	*Harrison Bardwell*
Crane, Stephen	*Johnston Smith*
Crayon, Geoffrey	**Washington Irving**
Creasey, John	*Gordon Ashe*
	M.E. Cooke
	Margaret Cooke
	Henry St. John Cooper
	Credo
	Norman Deane
	Elise Fecamps
	Robert Caine Frazer
	Patrick Gill
	Michael Halliday
	Charles Hogarth
	Brian Hope
	Colin Hughes
	Kyle Hunt
	Abel Mann
	Peter Manton
	J.J. Marric
	James Marsden
	Richard Martin
	Rodney Matheson
	Anthony Morton
	Ken Ranger
	William K. Reilly
	Tex Riley
	Henry St. John
	Jimmy Wilde
	Jeremy York
Credo	**John Creasey**
Crichton, Robert	*Robert Bridgeport*
Crisp, Quentin	**Dennis Pratt**
Cro-Cro	**Edward Alexander Crowley**
Cross, Mary Ann Evans	*George Eliot*
	Mary Ann (Marian) Evans
Cross, Stewart	**Harry Sinclair Drago**
Crow, Levi	**Manly Wade Wellman**
Crowley, Aleister	**Edward Alexander Crowley**
Crowley, (Edward) Aleister	**Edward Alexander Crowley**
Crowley, Edward Alexander	*St. E. of M. and S.A.*
	Abhavananda, Alastor (in Greek)
	Alastor le Demon du Solitude
	The Priest of the Princes Ankh-af-na-Khonsu
	Ariel
	Gerard Aumont
	The Authoress
	X', O.T.O. Ireland
	Iona and all... Baphomet
	The 666, 9'=2' A.'.A.'. Beast

Francis Bendick
George Archibald Bishop
Lord Boleskine
Algernon Robert Charles Brinburning
Madame Bock Brune
A.E.C., E.A.C., H.C., J.C., C.M. of the Vigilantes
Cain
Caligula
A Gentleman of the University of Cambridge
Candlestick
Cantab
The Reverend P.D. Carey
D. Carr
H.D. Carr
Cerebellum
Sir Meduim Coeli
Cor Scorpionis
Cro-Cro
(Edward) Aleister Crowley
Aleister Crowley
Robinson C. Crowley
Saint Edward Aleister
33', 90', X'... Crowley
Cyril Custance
DCLXVI
Marshal de Cambronne
Comte de Fenix
Barbay de Roche(c)h(o)uart
O Dhammaloyou
Adam Dias
Diogenes
Fra H.I. Edinburgh
V.
M.D. English
Felix
Percy Flage
Alice L. Foote
G.H.
O.M. Frater
A Gentile
Georgos
Laura Graham
James Grahame
Mrs. Bloomer Greymare
O.H.
Oliver Haddo
Hamlet
S.C. Hiller
A.C. Hobbs
S. Holmes
Jonathon
Natu Minimus Hutchinson
I.I., K.S.I.
Lemuel S. Innocent
Professor
Imperator Jacobus
K.H.A.K.
Edward Kelly
Dost Achiba Khan
Khaled Khan
Hodgson Y. Knott

Hsüan Ko, Ko Yuen
Sir Maurice E. Kulm
A.L.
Jeanne La Goulue
Nick Lamb
The Brothers Lazarus
LCLXVI
E. Le Roulx
Leo
Doris (Baby) Leslie
A London Physician
Major Lutiy
The Late Major Lutiy
O.M.
Macgregor of Boleskine and Abertarff
John, Junior Masefield
J.McC.
A Mental Traveller
Miles
S.J. Mills
Mohammed, Morpheus
A Mourner Clad In Green
Martial Nay
A New York Specialist
Percy W
P.R.A.S., P.H.B.S... Newlands
Hilda Norfolk
E.G.O.
Panurge
Enid, aged twelve Parsons
Percurabo
Perdurabo
Frater Perdurabo
Prater Perdurabo
Probationer
Prometheus
Prob Pudor
A. Quiller Jr.
Ethel Ramsay
John Roberts
The Author of Rosa Mundi
S.O.S.
H. Sapiens
William, pp. Ouija Board Shakespear
Mahatma Guru Sri Paramahansa Shivaji
Super Sinistram
Six Six Six (666)
The Prophet of the New Aeon Six Six Six (666)
John St. John
Count Vladimir Svaroff
H.K.T.
Alexander Tabasco
Eric Tait
M.S. Tarr
Logos Aionos (in Greek)
Thelema
Therion
The Master Therion
To Mega (in Greek)
DCLXVI Therion
David Thomas

Dekker, Eduard Douwes	*Multatuli*
de Kostrowitski, Wilhelm	*Guillaume Apollinaire*
de la Mare, Walter John	*Walter Ramal*
de la Ramée, (Marie) Louise	*Ouida*
de la Torre, Lillian	**Lillian (de la Torre Bueno) McCue**
DeLillo, Don	*Cleo Birdwell*
del Rey, Lester	**P(aul) W. Fairman**
Demijohn, Tho	**Thomas M(ichael) Disch and John T(homas) Sladek**
Deming, Kirk	**Harry Sinclair Drago**
de Natale, Francine	**Barry N(orman) Malzberg**
Denmark, Harrison	**Roger (Joseph) Zelazny**
Denny, Norman	*Bruce Norman*
Dent, Lester	*Maxwell Grant*
	Kenneth Roberts
	Kenneth Robeson
	Tim Ryan
Dentinger, Stephen	**Edward D(entinger) Hoch**
Derleth, August William	*Will Garth*
	Stephen Grendon
	Eldon Heath
	Kenyon Holmes
	J. Sheridan Le Fanu
	Tally Mason
	Michael West
de Roche(c)h(o)uart, Barbay	**Edward Alexander Crowley**
Dersonne, Jacques	**Georges Simenon**
De Voto, Bernard Augustine	*John August*
	Cady Hewes
	Cady Lewes
Dexter, John	**Marion Zimmer Bradley and John Coleman**
Dexter, Martin	**Frederick Schiller Faust**
Dhammaloyou, O	**Edward Alexander Crowley**
Dias, Adam	**Edward Alexander Crowley**
Di Bassetto, Corns	**George Bernard Shaw**
Dick, Philip K(indred)	*Richard Phillips*
Dickens, Charles	*Boz*
	Timothy Sparks
Dickenson, Carter	**John Dickson Carr**
Dickson, Carr	**John Dickson Carr**
Dickson, Carter	**John Dickson Carr**
Dietrich, Robert	**E(verette) Howard Hunt Jr.**
Dinesen, Isak	**Karen Christence Blixen-Finecke**
Diogenes	**Edward Alexander Crowley**
Diomede, John K.	**George Alec Effinger**
Disch, Thomas M(ichael)	*Thom Demijohn*
	Leonie Hargrave
	Cassandra Knye
d'Isly, Georges	**Georges Simenon**
Dissenter, A	**Jonathan Swift**
DiVono, Sharman	*Victor W. Appleton II*
Dixon, Thomas	*Burt Cole*
Doctor, The Good	**Isaac Asimov**
Dodgson, C(harles) L(utwidge)	*Lewis Carroll*
Doenim, Susan	**George Alec Effinger**
Dogyear, Drew	**Edward (St. John) Gorey**
Donovan, Dick	**James Edward Muddock**
Doolittle, Hilda	*Hilda Doolittle Aldington*
	H.D.
	John Helforth
Dorsage, Jean	**Georges Simenon**
Dorsan, Luc	**Georges Simenon**

Dossage, Jean	**Georges Simenon**
Dougherty, William	*Victor W. Appleton II*
Douglas, Leonard	**Ray(mond Douglas) Bradbury**
Douro, Marquis of	**Charlotte Brontë**
Dowdy, Mrs. Regera	**Edward (St. John) Gorey**
Doyle, Debra	*Victor W. Appleton II*
Doyle, John	**Harlan (Jay) Ellison** and **Robert (Ranke) Graves**
Dr. A	**Isaac Asimov**
Dr. Acula	**Forrest J. Ackerman**
Drago, Harry Sinclair	*Stewart Cross*
	Kirk Deming
	Will Ermine
	Bliss Lomax
	J. Wesley Putnam
	Grant Sinclair
Drapier, M.B.	**Jonathan Swift**
Dreadstone, Carl	**(John) Ramsey Campbell** and **Walter Harris**
Dresser, Davis	*Asa Baker*
	Matthew Blood
	Kathryn Culver
	Don Davis
	Hal Debrett
	Brett Halliday
	Anthony Scott
	Anderson Wayne
Droch	**Robert Bridges**
Dr. Seuss	**Theodor Seuss Geisel**
Drummond, Walter	**Robert Silverberg**
DuBois, Charles	**Mary Elizabeth Counselman**
Dufault, Joseph Ernest Nephtali	*Will James*
Dumas, Claudine	**Barry N(orman) Malzberg**
Duncan, David John	*Ken Hood*
Dunne, John L.	**H(oward) P(hillips) Lovecraft**
Dunsany, Lord	**Edward John Moreton Drax Plunkett**
Dunstan, Andrew	**A(rthur) Bertram Chandler**
du Perry, Jean	**Georges Simenon**
Dupin, Amandine-Aurore-Lucile	*George Sand*
	Jules Sand
Durham, David	**Roy (C.) Vickers**
Durrell, Lawrence (George)	*Charles Norden*
Dwyer, Deanna	**Dean (Ray) Koontz**
Dwyer, K.R.	**Dean (Ray) Koontz**
E., A.	**George William Russell**
Early, Jack	**Sandra Scoppettone**
E.B.W.	**E.B. White**
Eckman, F.R.	**Jan de Hartog**
Eckman, J. Forrester	**Forrest J(ames) Ackerman**
Eddy, Mary Baker	*Mary Baker Glover*
Edgy, Wardore	**Edward (St. John) Gorey**
Edinburgh, Fra H.I.	**Edward Alexander Crowley**
Edmonds, Paul	**Henry Kuttner**
Edwards, Norman	**Terry (Gene) Carr** and **Theodore Edward White**
Edwin, James	**James E(dwin) Gunn**
Effinger, George Alec	*John K. Diomede*
	Susan Doenim
Egan, Lesley	**(Barbara) Elizabeth Linington**
Egleton, Clive	*Patrick Blake*
	John Tarrant
Egremont, Michael	**Michael Harrison**
Eisner, Sam	**C(yril) M. Kornbluth**
Eisner, Simon	**C(yril) M. Kornbluth**

Elbertus, Fra	**Elbert Hubbard**
Eldred, Brian	**Ray(mond Douglas) Bradbury**
Elia	**Charles Lamb**
Eliot, George	**Mary Ann Evans Cross**
Elizabeth	**Countess Mary Annette Von Arnim Beauchamp Russell**
Elliott, Bruce	*Maxwell Grant*
Elliot(t), Don	**Robert Silverberg**
Elliott, William	**Ray(mond Douglas) Bradbury**
Ellis, Landon	**Harlan (Jay) Ellison**
Ellison, Harlan (Jay)	*Lee Archer*
	Cheech Beldone
	Phil Beldone
	C(ordwainer) Bird
	Jay Charby
	Robert Courtney
	Price Curtis
	John Doyle
	Wallace Edmondson
	Landon Ellis
	Sley Harson
	Ellis Hart
	E.K. Jarvis
	Ivar Jorgenson
	Al Maddern
	John Magnus
	Paul Merchant
	Clyde Mitchell
	Nalrah (Nabrah?) Nosille
	Bert Parker
	Ellis Robertson
	Pat Roeder
	Jay Solo
	Derry Tiger
	Harlan White
Elron	**L(a Fayette) Ron(ald) Hubbard Sr.**
Emsh	**Edward A. Emshwiller**
Emshwiller, Edward A.	*Ed Alexander*
	Emsler
	Emsh
	Willer
Emsler	**Edward A. Emshwiller**
Englehardt, Frederick	**L(a Fayette) Ron(ald) Hubbard Sr.**
English, V., M.D.	**Edward Alexander Crowley**
Epernay, Mark	**John Kenneth Galbraith**
Ericson, Walter	**Howard (Melvin) Fast**
Erman, Jacques de Forrest	**Forrest J(ames) Ackerman**
Ermann, Jack	**Forrest J(ames) Ackerman**
Ermine, Will	**Harry Sinclair Drago**
Ernst, Paul (Frederick)	*George Alden Edson*
	Kenneth Robeson
	Paul Frederick Stern
Esterbrook, Tom	**L(a Fayette) Ron(ald) Hubbard Sr.**
Esteven (Estevan?), John	**Samuel Shellabarger**
Eustace, Robert	**Eustace Robert Barton**
Evans, E. Everett	*Harry J. Gardner*
	H.E. Verett
Evans, Evan	**Frederick Schiller Faust** and **Alan Stoker**
Evans, Mary Ann (Marian)	**Mary Ann Evans Cross**
Everson, William	*Brother Antonius*
Ewing, Frederick R.	**Jean Shepherd** and **Edward Hamilton Waldo**
Fabian, Warner	**Samuel Hopkins Adams**

Fair, A.A.	**Erle Stanley Gardner**
Fairbairn, Roger	**John Dickson Carr**
Fairman, P(aul) W.	*Adam Chase*
	Lester del Rey
	Clee Garson
	E.K. Jarvis
	Ivar Jorgensen
	Robert (Eggert) Lee
	Paul Lohrman
	F.W. Paul
	Mallory Storm
	Gerald Vance
Falconer, Kenneth	**C(yril) M. Kornbluth**
Falk, Lee	**Basil Copper**
Farigoule, Louis	*Jules Romains*
Farley, Ralph (Milne)	**Roger S(herman) Hoar**
Farmer, Philip José	*Cordwainer Bird*
	Paul Chapin
	Maxwell Grant
	Dane Helstrom
	Rod Keen
	Harry 'Bunny' Manders
	William Norfolk
	Kenneth Robeson
	Jonathan Swift Somers III
	Leo Queequeg Tincrowder
	Kilgore Trout
	John H. Watson MD
Farr, John	**Jack Webb**
Farrell, James T(homas)	*Jonathan Titulesco Fogarty*
Farrell, John Wade	**John D(ann) MacDonald**
Farren, Richard M.	**(Sir) John Betjeman**
Fast, Howard (Melvin)	*E.V. Cunningham*
	Walter Ericson
	Simon Kent
Faulcon, Robert	**Robert (Paul) Holdstock**
Faulkner, William (Cuthbert)	*Ernest V. Trueblood*
Faust, Alexander	**Harry Altshuler**
Faust, Frederick Schiller	*Frank Austin*
	George Owen Baxter
	Lee Bolt
	Max Brand
	Walter C. Butler
	George Challis
	Peter Dawson
	Martin Dexter
	Evin Evan
	Evan Evans
	John Frederick
	Frederick Frost
	Dennis Lawton
	David Manning
	Peter Henry Morland
	Hugh Owen
	John Schoolcraft
	Nicholas Silver
	Henry Uriel
	Peter Ward
Fawkes, Farrah	**Andrew J(efferson V.) Offutt**
Fawkes, Guy	**Robert Benchley**
Feinstein, Isidor	*I.F. Stone*

Felix	**Edward Alexander Crowley**
Fenimore, W.	**A(braham Grace) Merritt**
Fenn, Lionel	**Charles L(ewis) Grant**
Fernandes	**Joyce Carol Oates**
Ferney, Manuel	**Manly Wade Wellman**
Ferrat, Jacques Jean	**Sam(uel Kimball) Merwin Jr.**
Fetzer, Herman	*Jake Falstaff*
Fickling, Forrest E.	*G.G. Fickling*
Fickling, G.G.	**Forrest E. Fickling and Gloria Fickling**
Fickling, Gloria	*G.G. Fickling*
Field, Gans T.	**Manly Wade Wellman**
Finney, Jack	**Walter Braden Finney**
Finney, Walter Braden	*Jack Finney*
Fips, Mohammed U(lysses) S(ocrates)	**Hugo Gernsback**
Firth, Violet M(ary)	*Dion Fortune*
Fish, Robert L(loyd)	*A.C. Lamprey*
	Robert L. Pike
	Lawrence Roberts
Fiske, Tarleton	**Robert (Albert) Bloch**
Fitzgerald, Hugh	**L(yman) Frank Baum**
Flage, Percy	**Edward Alexander Crowley**
Flapdoodle, Phineas	**Henry Miller**
Fleck, Betty	**Lauran Paine**
Fleming, Dorothy Leigh Sayers	**Dorothy L(eigh) Sayers**
Fletcher, George U.	**(Murray) Fletcher Pratt**
Flower, Jessie Graham	**Josephine Chase**
Fodor, Nancy	**Hereward Carrington**
Foe, Daniel	*Daniel DeFoe*
Fogarty, Jonathan Titulesco	**James T(homas) Farrell**
Folke, Will	**Robert (Albert) Bloch**
Follett, Ken(neth Martin)	*Martin Martinsen*
	Simon Myles
	Zachary Stone
Foote, Alice L.	**Edward Alexander Crowley**
Ford, Ford Madox	**Ford Madox Hueffer**
Forrest, Julian	**Edward Wagenknecht**
Fortune, Dione	**Violet M(ary) Firth**
Fosse, Harold C.	**H(orace) L(eonard) Gold**
Foster, Alan Dean	*George Lucas*
Fountain, Arnold	**(Charles) Fulton Oursler**
France, Anatole	**Jacques-Anatole-François Thibault**
Franklin, Madeleine L'Engle Camp	*Madeleine L'Engle*
Fraser, Jane	**Rosamunde Pilcher**
Frazer, Andrew	**Milton Lesser**
Frazer, Robert Caine	**John Creasey**
Frazier, Arthur	**(Henry) Kenneth Bulmer and Laurence James**
Frederick, Jo	**Milward Rodon Kennedy Burge and Frederick Schiller Faust**
Freeling, Nic(h)olas	*F.R.E. Nicholas*
Freeman, Mary E(leanor) Wilkins	*Mary Wilkins*
	Mary E(leanor) Wilkins-Freeman
Freeman, R(ichard) Austin	*Clifford Ashdown*
French, Paul	**Isaac Asimov**
Friedan, Betty	**Betty Naomi Goldstein**
Frikell, Samri	**(Charles) Fulton Oursler**
Frost, Frederick	**Frederick Schiller Faust**
Fuentes, Carlos	**Carlos Manuel Fuentes Macías**
Furey, Michael	**Arthur (Henry) Sarsfield Ward**
Gaite, Francis	**Cyril H(enry) Coles and Adelaide F(rancis) O(ke) Manning**
Galbraith, John Kenneth	*Mark Epernay*
Ganpat	**Martin Louis Alan Gompertz**
Gardner, Craig Shaw	**Edgar Rice Burroughs**

Gardner, Erle Stanley	*A.A. Fair*
	Charles M. Green
	Grant Holiday
	Carleton Kendrake
	Charles J. Kenn(e)y
	Robert Park
	Robert Parr
	Les Tillray
Gardner, Harry J.	**E. Everett Evans**
Gardner, Miriam	**Marion Zimmer Bradley**
Gardner, Noel	**Henry Kuttner**
Garis, Howard R.	*Victor Appleton*
Garrett, Gordon	**(Gordon) Randall (Phillip David) Garrett**
Garrett, (Gordon) Randall (Phillip David)	*Gordon Aghill*
	Grandal Barretton
	Alexander Blade
	Alfred Blake
	Andrew Blake
	Walter Bupp
	Ralph Burke
	Gordon Garrett
	David Gordon
	Richard Greer
	Larry Mark Harris
	Laurence M. Janifer
	Ivar Jorgenson
	Darrel T. Langart
	Blake MacKenzie
	Seaton Mckettrig
	Clyde (T.) Mitchell
	Mark Phillips
	Robert Randall
	Leonard G. Spencer
	S.M. Tenneshaw
	Gerald Vance
	Barbara Wilson
Garrison, Frederick	**Upton Sinclair**
Garron, Robert A.	**Howard E(lmer) Wandrei**
Garve, Andrew	**Paul Winterton**
Gash, Jonathan	**John Grant MD.**
Gashbuck, Greno	**Hugo Gernsback**
Gaunt, Graham	**John Grant MD.**
Gaylord, Timeus	**Clark Ashton Smith**
Geiger, Hansruedi	*H.R. Geiger*
Geiger, H.R.	**Hansruedi Geiger**
Geisel, Ted	**Theodor Seuss Geisel**
Geisel, Theodor Seuss	*Ted Geisel*
	Theo Le Sieg
	Dr. Seuss
Genius	**Charlotte Brontë**
Gentile, A	**Edward Alexander Crowley**
Georgos	**Edward Alexander Crowley**
Gérôme	**Jacques-Anatole-François Thibault**
Geralda, Lady	**Anne Brontë**
Gernsback, Hugo	*Grego Barshuck*
	Mohammed U(lysses) S(ocrates) Fips
	Greno Gashbuck
	Gus N. Habergock
	Baron Munchausen
Giles, Geoffrey	**Forrest J(ames) Ackerman** and **Walter Gillings**
Giles, Gordon A.	**Earl Andrew Binder** and **Otto O(scar) Binder**

Gill, Patrick	**John Creasey**
Giovanni, Nikki	**Yolande C. Giovanni**
Giovanni, Yolande C.	*Nikki Giovanni*
Gissing, George	**J. Storer Glouston**
Glidden, Frederick (Dilley)	*Luke Short*
Glouston, J. Storer	*George Gissing*
Glover, Mary Baker	**Mary Baker Eddy**
Gold, H(orace) L(eonard)	*Clyde Crane Campbell*
	Dudley Dell
	Harold C. Fosse
	Julian Graey
	Leigh Keith
Goldman, William	*Harry Longbaugh*
	S. Morgenstern
Goldsmith, Oliver	*James Willington*
Goldstein, Betty Naomi	*Betty Friedan*
Gompertz, Martin Louis Alan	*Ganpat*
Good Doctor, The	**Isaac Asimov**
Gordon, Charles William	*Ralph Connor*
Gordon, David	**(Gordon) Randall (Phillip David) Garrett**
Gordon, Verne	**Donald A(llen) Wollheim**
Gorki [Gorky], Maxim	**Aleksei Maksimovich Pyeshkov**
Gorman, Beth	**Lauran Paine**
Goryan, Sirak	**William Saroyan**
Goudeket, Mme Maurice	**Sidonie-Gabrielle Colette**
Goulart, Ron(ald Joseph)	*Josephine Kains*
	Jill Kearny
	Julian Kearny
	Howard Lee
	Kenneth Robeson
	Frank S. Shawn
	Joseph Silva
	Con Steffanson]
Gould, Alan	**Victor Canning**
Grady, Tex	**Jack Webb**
Graey, Julian	**H(orace) L(eonard) Gold**
Graham, Laura	**Edward Alexander Crowley**
Graham, Tom	**(Harry) Sinclair Lewis**
Grahame, James	**Edward Alexander Crowley**
Grandower, Elissa	**Hillary (Baldwin) Waugh**
Grant, Charles L(ewis)	*Felicia Andrews*
	Steven Charles
	Lionel Fenn
	Simon Lake
	Deborah Lewis
	Geoffrey L. Marsh
Grant, Joan	**Joan Marshall Kelsey**
Grant, John, MD.	*Jonathan Gash*
	Graham Gaunt
	Jonathan Grant
Grant, Maxwell	**Lester Dent**
	Bruce Elliott
	Philip José Farmer
	Walter B(rown) Gibson
	Dennis Lynds
	Theodore Tinsley
Grant, Steven	*Victor W. Appleton II*
Graves. Robert (Ranke)	*John Doyle*
	Barbara Rich
	Frank Richards
Graves, Valerie	**Marion Zimmer Bradley**

Gray, Anthony	**Ernest K(ellogg) Gann**
Grayson, David	**Ray Stannard Baker**
Greaves, Richard	**George Barr McCutcheon**
Greaves, Robert	**George Barr McCutcheon**
Green, Charles M.	**Erle Stanley Gardner**
Greer, Germaine	*Rose Blight*
Greer, Richard **(Gordon) Randall (Phillip David) Garrett and Robert Silverberg**	
Gregory, Stephan	**Don(ald Eugene) Pendleton**
Grendon, Stephen	**August William Derleth**
Grenville, Pelham	**P(elham) G(renville) Wodehouse**
Grey, Carol	**Robert (Augustine) W(ard) Lowndes**
Greymare, Mrs. Bloomer	**Edward Alexander Crowley**
Grile, Dod	**Ambrose (Gwinnett) Bierce**
Grinnell, David	**Donald A(llen) Wollheim**
Grode, Redway	**Edward (St. John) Gorey**
Groener, Carl	**Robert (Augustine) W(ard) Lowndes**
Guernsey, H.W.	**Howard E(lmer) Wandrei**
Gunn, James E(dwin)	*James Edwin*
	Edwin James
Gut, Gom	**Georges Simenon**
Guthrie, Thomas Anstey	*F. Anstey*
	Hope Bandoff
	William Monarch Jones
Gwendolyn, Jacob Tonson	**Arnold Bennett**
H., E.W.	**E(rnest) W(illiam) Hornung**
H., H.	**Helen (Maria Fiske) Hunt Jackson**
H., O.	**Edward Alexander Crowley**
Habergock, Gus N.	**Hugo Gernsback**
Haddo, Oliver	**Edward Alexander Crowley**
Haldeman, Joe W(illiam)	*Robert Graham*
Hale, Edward Everett	*J. Thomas Darragh*
	Frederic Ingham
	New England minister
Hall, James	**Henry Kuttner**
Halliday, Brett	**Davis Dresser**
	William John Pronzini
Halliday, Michael	**John Creasey**
Hamilton, Clive	**C(live) S(taples) Lewis**
Hamlet	**Edward Alexander Crowley**
Hammett, Samuel Dashiell	*Peter Collinson*
Hammond, Keith	**Henry Kuttner and C(atherine) L(ucille) Moore**
Hammond, Ralph	**(Ralph) Hammond Innes**
Hannon, Ezra	**Salvatore A. Lombino**
Harford, Henry	**W(illiam) H(enry) Hudson**
Hargrave, Leonie	**Thomas M(ichael) Disch**
Harker, Jonathan	**Joe R. Lansdale**
Harris, Frank	**John Thomas Harris**
Harris, J.B.	**John Wyndham Parkes Lucas Beynon Harris**
Harris, Joel Chandler	*Uncle Remus*
Harris, Johnson	**John Wyndham Parkes Lucas Beynon Harris**
Harris, John Thomas	*Frank Harris*
Harris, John Wyndham Parkes Lucas Beynon	*John Beynon*
	J.B. Harris
	Johnson Harris
	Max Hennessy
	Lucas Parker
	Lucas Parkes
	Wyndham Parkes
	John Windham
	John Wyndam
	John Wyndham

Harrison, Bruce	**Edgar Pangborn**
Harrison, Chip	**Lawrence Block**
Harson, Sley	**Harlan (Jay) Ellison**
Hart, Ellis	**Harlan (Jay) Ellison**
Hastings, Hudson	**Henry Kuttner** and **C(atherine) L(ucille) Moore**
Hawkins, Sir Anthony Hope	*Anthony Hope*
Haygood, G. Arnold	**Frank G(ill) Slaughter**
H.D.	**Hilda Doolittle**
Heard, Gerald	**H(enry) F(itzgerald) Heard**
Heard, H(enry) F(itzgerald)	*Gerald Heard*
Hearn, Lafcadio	*Yakumo Koizumi*
Heath, Eldon	**August William Derleth**
Heinlein, Robert Anson	*Anson MacDonald*
	Lyle Monroe
	John Riverside
	Caleb Saunders
	Elma Wentz
	Simon York
Heldmann, Richard B(ernard)	*Richard Marsh*
Helstrom, Dane	**Philip José Farmer**
Hemingway, Ernest	*Morgan Llywelyn*
Hennessy, Max	**John Wyndham Parkes Lucas Beynon Harris**
Edgar Henry	**Albion W(inegar) Tourgée**
Henry, O.	**William Sydney Porter**
Heritage, Martin	**Sydney Horler**
Herman, William	**Ambrose (Gwinnett) Bierce**
Herriott, James	**J.A. Wight**
Herron, Edna	*Ben Aronin*
Hershfield, Harry	**Walter B(rown) Gibson**
Herzog, Emile Salomon Wilhelm	*André Maurois*
Higgins, Jack	**Henry Patterson**
Hiller, S.C.	**Edward Alexander Crowley**
Hill-Lutz, Grace Livingston	*Grace Livingston*
	Marcia Macdonald
Hilton, James	*Glen Trevor*
Hindin, Nathan	**Robert (Albert) Bloch**
Hirschfield, Magnus	**Arthur Koestler**
Hobbs, A.C.	**Edward Alexander Crowley**
Hodemart, Peter	**Pierre Audemars**
Hogarth	**Rockwell Kent**
Hogarth, Charles	**(Ivor) Ian Bowen** and **John Creasey**
Holding, James	*Ellery Queen Jr.*
Holiday, Grant	**Erle Stanley Gardner**
Hollerbochen	**Ray(mond Douglas) Bradbury**
Holley, Marietta	*Josiah Allen's Wife*
	Samantha Allen
Holmes, Gordon	**M(atthew) P(hipps) Shiel**
	Louis Tracy
Holmes, Kenyon	**August William Derleth**
Holmes, S.	**Edward Alexander Crowley**
Holt, Harmony	**William Rotsler**
Holt, Samuel	**D(onald) E(dwin) Westlake**
Hope, Anthony	**Sir Anthony Hope Hawkins**
Hope, Brian	**John Creasey**
Hopley, George	**Cornell George Hopley-Woolrich**
Hopley-Woolrich, Cornell George	*George Hopley*
	William Irish
	Cornell Woolrich
Horn, Gertrude Franklin	**Gertrude Franklin (Horn) Atherton**
Horn, Peter	**C(yril) M. Kornbluth, Henry Kuttner** and **D(avid) Vern**
Hoskin, Cyril Henry	*T. Lopsang Rampa*

House, Brian	**Robert Ludlum**
Howard, Robert E(rvin)	*Patrick Ervin*
	Patrick Howard
	Patrick Irvin
	Sam Walser
	Robert Ward
Howard, Warren F.	**Frederik (George) Pohl (Jr.)**
Hubbard, Cal	**Elbert Hubbard**
Hubbard, Elbert	*Fra Elbertus*
	Cal Hubbard
Hubbard, L(a Fayette) Ron(ald), Sr.	*Elron*
	Frederick Englehardt
	Tom Esterbrook
	Rene Lafayette
	Capt. B.A. Northrop
	Kurt von Rachen
Hudson, Jeffrey	**(John) Michael Crichton**
Hueffer, Ford Hermann	**Ford Madox Hueffer**
Hueffer, Ford Madox	*Daniel Chaucer*
	Ford Madox Ford
	Fenil Haig
	Ford Hermann Hueffer
Hughes, Colin	**John Creasey**
Hughes, Sylvia	**Sylvia Plath**
Hunt, Kyle	**John Creasey**
Hunter, Evan	**Salvatore A. Lombino**
Hutchinson, Jonathon, Natu Minimus	**Edward Alexander Crowley**
I., I.	**Edward Alexander Crowley**
I., K.S.	**Edward Alexander Crowley**
Iddrissyeh, Achmed Abdullah	**Alexander Nicholayevitch Romanoff**
Iles, Frances	**A(nthony) B(erkeley) Cox**
Incogniteau, Jean-Louis	**Jack Kerouac**
Ingham, Frederic	**Edward Everett Hale**
Ingoldsby, Thomas	**Richard Barham**
Innes, Michael	**J(ohn) I(nnes) M(ackintosh) Stewart**
Innes, (Ralph) Hammond	*Ralph Hammond*
Innocent, Lemuel S.	**Edward Alexander Crowley**
Irish, William	**Cornell George Hopley-Woolrich**
Irvin, Patrick	**Robert E(rvin) Howard**
Irving, Washington	*Geoffrey Crayon*
	Diedrich Knickerbocker
	Launcelot Langstaff
	Jonathan Oldstyle
Isherwood, Christopher	**William Bradshaw**
Ives, Morgan	**Marion Zimmer Bradley**
Jackson, Helen (Maria Fiske) Hunt	*H.H.*
	Saxe Holm
Jacob, Piers Anthony Dillingham	*Piers Anthony*
	Pier Xanthony
Jacobus, Professor, Imperator	**Edward Alexander Crowley**
Jakes, John (William)	*Darius John Granger*
	Alan Payne
	Jay Scotland
	Jay Scotland
	Allen Wilder
James, Edwin	**James E(dwin) Gunn**
James, P(hyllis) D(orothy)	*Phyllis White*
James, Will	**Joseph Ernest Nephtali Dufault**
Janifer, Laurence M.	**(Gordon) Randall (Phillip David) Garrett**
Janson, Hank	**Harry Hobson and Michael (John) Moorcock**
Jeake, Samuel	**Conrad (Potter) Aiken**

Jefferson, Henry Lee	**James Branch Cabell**
Jennings, Gary	*Gabriel Quyth*
Jessel, John	**Stanley G(rauman) Weinbaum**
J.K.B.	**John Kendrick Bangs**
John, David St.	**E(verette) Howard Hunt, Jr.**
John, Henry St.	**John Creasey**
Johnson, Benj(amin) F.	**James Whitcomb Riley**
Johnson, Martha	**Elizabeth Lansing**
Johnson, Mel	**Barry N(orman) Malzberg**
Jones, James Athearn	*Matthew Murgatroyd*
Jones, Leroy	*Imamu Amiri Baraka*
Jones, Raymond F.	*David Anderson*
Jones, William Monarch	**Thomas Anstey Guthrie**
Josephs, Henry	**Robert (Augustine) W(ard) Lowndes**
Josiah Allen's Wife	**Marietta Holley**
Jouvenal, Mme Henri de	**Sidonie-Gabrielle Colette**
J.T.	**Eric Temple Bell**
Judd, Cyril (M.)	**Josephine Juliet Grossman** and **C(yril) M. Kornbluth**
K., K.H.A.	**Edward Alexander Crowley**
Kaiine, Tanith Lee	*Tanith Lee*
Kain, Saul	**Siegfried Sassoon**
Kains, Josephine	**Ron(ald Joseph) Goulart**
Kaler, James Otis	*James Otis*
Kane, Wilson	**Robert (Albert) Bloch**
Karageorge, Michael	**Poul (William) Anderson**
Kastel, Warren	**C(hester) S. Geier** and **Robert Silverberg**
Kavanagh, Paul	**Lawrence Block**
Kearny, Jill	**Ron(ald Joseph) Goulart**
Kearny, Julian	**Ron(ald Joseph) Goulart**
Keefe, Jack	**Ring Lardner Jr.**
Keen, Rod	**Philip José Farmer**
Keiber, Fritz	**Fritz (Reuter) Leiber Jr.**
Keith, Leigh	**H(orace) L(eonard) Gold**
Kelly, Edward	**Edward Alexander Crowley**
Kelsey, Joan Marshall	*Joan Grant*
Kendrake, Carleton	**Erle Stanley Gardner**
Kennerley, Thomas	*Tom Wolfe*
Kenn(e)y, Charles J.	**Erle Stanley Gardner**
Kent, Kelv	**A(rthur) K(elvin) Barnes, C(yril) M. Kornbluth** and **Henry Kuttner**
Kent, Mallory	**Robert (Augustine) W(ard) Lowndes**
Kent, Rockwell	*Hogarth Jr.*
Kent, Simon	**Max Catto** and **Howard (Melvin) Fast**
Kenton, Maxwell	**Terry Southern** and **Mason Hoffenberg**
Kenyon, Robert O.	**Henry Kuttner**
Kerouac, Jack (Jean-Louis Lebrid)	*Jean-Louis Incognitea*
Kerr, Ben	**William (Thomas) Ard**
Khan, Dost Achiba	**Edward Alexander Crowley**
Khan, Khaled	**Edward Alexander Crowley**
Kim	**Georges Simenon**
Kineji, Maborushi	**Walter B(rown) Gibson**
King, Stephen (Edwin)	*Richard Bachman*
	John Swithen
Kingsley, Charles	*Parson Lot*
Kjelgaard, James Arthur	*Jim Kjelgaard*
Kjelgaard, Jim	**Robert (Albert) Bloch** and **James Arthur Kjelgaard**
Klass, Philip (J.)	*Kenneth Putnam*
	William Tenn
Klausner, Amos	*Amos Oz*
Knickerbocker, Diedrich	**Washington Irving**
Knight, David	**Richard S(cott) Prather**
Knott, Hodgson Y.	**Edward Alexander Crowley**

Knowles, William	*Clyde Allison*
	Clyde Ames
Knox, Calvin M.	**Robert Silverberg**
Knye, Cassandra	**Thomas M(ichael) Disch** and **John T(homas) Sladek**
Ko, Hsüan	**Edward Alexander Crowley**
Koestler, Arthur	*A. Costler*
	Magnus Hirschfield
	Vigil
Koizumi, Yakumo	**Lafcadio Hearn**
Konigsberg, Allen Stewart	*Woody Allen*
Koontz, Dean (Ray)	*David Axton*
	Leonard Chris
	Brian Coffey
	Deanna Dwyer
	K.R. Dwyer
	John Hill
	Leigh Nichols
	Anthony North
	Richard Paige
	Owen West
	Aaron Wolfe
Kornbluth, C(yril) M.	*Gabriel Barclay*
	Edward J. Bellin
	Arthur Cooke
	Cecil Corwin
	Walter C. Davies
	Sam Eisner
	Simon Eisner
	Kenneth Falconer
	Will Garth
	S.D. Gottesman
	Peter Horn
	Cyril (M.) Judd
	Kelvin Kent
	Paul Dennis Lavond
	Scott Mariner
	Lawrence O'Donnell
	Jordan Park
	Martin Pearson
	Ivar Towers
	Dirk Wylie
Korzeniowski, Jósef Teodor Konrad	*Joseph Conrad*
Kosinski, Jerzy (Nikodem)	*Joseph Novak*
Ko Yuen	**Edward Alexander Crowley**
Kulm, Sir Maurice E.	**Edward Alexander Crowley**
Kurtz, Wolfgang	**John (Kilian Houston) Brunner**
Kuttner, Henry	*Edward J. Bellin*
	Paul Edmonds
	Noel Gardner
	Will Garth
	James Hall
	Keith Hammond
	Hudson Hastings
	Peter Horn
	Kelvin Kent
	Robert O. Kenyon
	C.H. Liddell
	Hugh Maepenn
	K.H. Maepenn
	Scott Morgan
	Lawrence O'Donnell

	Lewis Padgett
	Woodrow Wilson Smith
	Charles Stoddard
L., A.	**Edward Alexander Crowley**
Lafayette, Rene	**L(a Fayette) Ron(ald) Hubbard Sr.**
La Goulue, Jeanne	**Edward Alexander Crowley**
Lake, Simon	**Charles L(ewis) Grant**
Lamb, Charles	*Elia*
Lamb, Nick	**Edward Alexander Crowley**
LaMoore, Louis Dearborn	*Tex Burns*
	Louis L'Amour
	Jim Mayo
L'Amour, Louis	**Louis Dearborn LaMoore**
Lamprey, A.C.	**Robert L(loyd) Fish**
Lang, Andrew	*A Huge Longway*
Langart, Darrel T.	**(Gordon) Randall (Phillip David) Garrett**
Lange, John	**(John) Michael Crichton**
Langstaff, Launcelot	**Washington Irving**
	James Kirk Paulding
Lansdale, Joe R.	*M. Dean Bayer*
	Jack Buchanan
	Richard Dale
	Jonathan Harker
	Mark Simmons
	Ray Slater
Lansing, Elizabeth	*Martha Johnson*
Lantern, The	**Don(ald Robert Perry) Marquis**
Lardner, Ring, Jr.	*Jack Keefe*
	Philip Rush
	Old Wilmer
Lasly, Walt	**Frederik (George) Pohl (Jr.)**
Latham, Philip	**Robert S(hirley) Richardson**
Lathrop, Francis	**Fritz (Reuter) Leiber Jr.**
Latimer, Jonathan (Wyatt)	*Peter Coffin*
la Torre, Lillian de	**Lillian McCue**
Laumer, (John) Keith	*Anthony Lebaron*
Laurieres, Chrisophe des	**Clark Ashton Smith**
Laverty, Donald	**James (Benjamin) Blish and Damon (Francis) Knight**
Lavington, Hubert	**Hereward Carrington**
Lawless, Anthony	**Philip MacDonald**
Lawrence, D(avid) H(erbert)	*Lawrence H. Davidson*
Lawrence, James Duncan	*Victor W. Appleton II*
Lawton, Dennis	**Frederick Schiller Faust**
Lazarus, The Brothers	**Edward Alexander Crowley**
LCLXVI	**Edward Alexander Crowley**
Learsi, Rufus	**Shalom Asch and Israel Goldberg**
Lebaron, Anthony	**(John) Keith Laumer**
LeCarré, John	**David John Moore Cornwell**
Lee, Andrew	**Louis Auchincloss**
Lee, Gypsy Rose	**Georgiana Ann Randolph**
Lee, Tanith	**Tanith Lee Kaiine**
Lee, Willy (William)	**William S. Burroughs**
Leiber, Fritz (Reuter), Jr.	*Fritz Keiber*
	Francis Lathrop
Leinster, Murray	**Will(iam) F(itzgerald) Jenkins**
L'Engle, Madeleine	**Madeleine L'Engle Camp Franklin**
Leo	**Edward Alexander Crowley**
	Sean O'Casey
Lepovsky, Manfred Bennington	*Manford B. Lee*
	Ellery Queen
	Barnaby Ross

Le Roulx, E.	**Edward Alexander Crowley**
Le Sieg, Theo	**Theodor Seuss Geisel**
Leslie, Doris (Baby)	**Edward Alexander Crowley**
Lesser, Milton	*Adam Chase*
	Andrew Frazer
	Darius John Granger
	Stephen Marlowe
	Jason Ridgway
	S.M. Tenneshaw
	C.H. Thames
Lessing, Doris (May)	*Jane Somers*
Lester, Irwin	**(Murray) Fletcher Pratt**
Levi, Eliphas	**Alphonse L. Constant**
Lewes, Cady	**Bernard Augustine De Voto**
Lewis, C(ecil) D(ay)	*Nicholas Blake*
Lewis, C(live) S(taples)	*N.W. Clerk*
	Clive Hamilton
	Jack Lewis
	N.W.
Lewis, D.B. Wyndham	*Timothy Shy*
Lewis, Deborah	**Charles L(ewis) Grant**
Lewis, (Harry) Sinclair	*Tom Graham*
Lewis, Jack	**C(live) S(taples) Lewis**
Ley, Willy	*Robert Willey*
Lin, Frank	**Gertrude Franklin (Horn) Atherton**
Linington, (Barbara) Elizabeth	*Anne Blaisdell*
	Lesley Egan
	Egan O'Neill
	Dell Shannon
Littlewit, Humphrey	**H(oward) P(hillips) Lovecraft**
Lockeridge, Frances & Richard	**Frances Louise Davis** and **Richard Orson**
Lofts, Nora	*Juliet Astley*
	Peter Curtis
Logue, Christopher	*Count Palmiro Vicarion*
Lomax, Bliss	**Harry Sinclair Drago**
Lombino, Salvatore A.	*John Abbott*
	Curt Cannon
	Hunt Collins
	Ezra Hannon
	Evan Hunter
	Richard Marsten
	Ed McBain
London, Jack	**John Griffith Chaney**
Long, Frank Belknap, Jr.	*Lyda Belknap Long*
	Leslie Northern
Long, Lyda Belknap	**Frank Belknap Long Jr.**
Longbaugh, Harry	**William Goldman**
Longway, A Huge	**Andrew Lang**
Loring, Peter	**Samuel Shellabarger**
Lorraine, Alden	**Forrest J(ames) Ackerman**
Lot, Parson	**Charles Kingsley**
Lothrop, Harriet M.	*Margaret Sydney*
Loti, Pierre	**L.M. Julien Viaud**
Lovecraft, H(oward) P(hillips)	*Laurence Appleton*
	John L. Dunne
	Humphrey Littlewit
	Archibald Maynwaring
	H(enry) Paget-Lowe
	Richard Raleigh
	Ames Dorrance Rowley
	Theobaldus Senectissimus

Macgregor of Boleskine and Abertarff	**Edward Alexander Crowley**
Machen, Arthur	*Leolinus Siluriensis*
Macías, Carlos Manuel Fuentes	*Carlos Fuentes*
McInerny, Ralph (Matthew)	*Edward Mackin*
	Monica Quill
MacIntrye, F. Gwynplaine	*Victor W. Appleton II*
MacKay, Mary	*Marie Corelli*
McKenna, Bridget	*Victor W. Appleton II*
McKenna, Richard	*Victor W. Appleton II*
MacKenzie, Blake	**(Gordon) Randall (Phillip David) Garrett**
McKenzie, Ray	**Robert Silverberg**
Mckettrig, Seaton	**(Gordon) Randall (Phillip David) Garrett**
Mackin, Edward	**Ralph (Matthew) McInerny**
MacLeod, Austin	**William MacLeod Raine**
McNeile, H(erman) C(yril)	*Sapper*
McQuay, Mike	*Victor W. Appleton II*
Maddern, Al	**Harlan (Jay) Ellison**
Maepenn, Hugh	**Henry Kuttner**
Maepenn, K.H.	**Henry Kuttner**
Magnus, John	**Harlan (Jay) Ellison**
Malcom, Dan	**Robert Silverberg**
Mallory, Drew	**Brian (Francis Wynne) Garfield**
Mallowan, Agatha Christie	**Agatha (Mary Clarissa Miller) Christie**
Malone, Sherry	**Robert (Albert) Bloch**
Malzberg, Barry N(orman)	*Mike Barry*
	Francine de Natale
	Claudine Dumas
	Mel Johnson
	Howard Lee
	Lee W. Mason
	K.M. O'Donnell Jr.
	Gerrold Watkins
Manders, Harry 'Bunny'	**Philip José Farmer**
Mann, Abel	**John Creasey**
Manning, Adelaide F(rancis) O(ke)	*Manning Coles*
	Francis Gaite
Manning, David	**Frederick Schiller Faust**
Manton, Peter	**John Creasey**
Maras, Karl	**(Henry) Kenneth Bulmer and Peter Hawkins**
March, Maxwell	**Margery Louise Allingham**
Mariner, Scott	**C(yril) M. Kornbluth and Frederik (George) Pohl**
Markham, Robert	**(Sir) Kingsley (William) Amis**
Marlowe, Stephen	**Milton Lesser**
Marner, Robert	**Algirdas Jonas Budrys**
Marquis, Don(ald Robert Perry)	*The Lantern*
	The Sundial
Marric, J.J.	**William Vivian Butler**
	John Creasey
Marsden, James	**John Creasey**
Marsh, Geoffrey L.	**Charles L(ewis) Grant**
Marsten, Richard	**Salvatore A. Lombino**
Martin, Richard	**John Creasey**
Martin, Webber	**Robert Silverberg**
Martin-Georges, Georges	**Georges Simenon**
Martinsen, Martin	**Ken(neth Martin) Follett**
Masefield, John, Junior	**Edward Alexander Crowley**
Marvel, Ik	**Donald G(rant) Mitchell**
Mason, Ernest	**Frederik (George) Pohl (Jr.)**
Mason, Ernst	**Frederik (George) Pohl (Jr.)**
Mason, Frank	**Algirdas Jonas Budrys**
Mason, F(rank) van Wyck	*Geoffrey Coffin*

	Frank W. Mason
	Ward Weaver
Mason, Frank W.	**F(rank) van Wyck Mason**
Mason, Lee W.	**Barry N(orman) Malzberg**
Mason, Mason Jordon	**Judson Crews**
Mason, Michael	**Edgar Smith**
Mason, Tally	**August William Derleth**
Masterson, Whit	**Bill Miller and Robert (Bob) Wade**
Master Therion	**Edward Alexander Crowley**
Matheson, Chris	**Richard Christian Matheson**
Matheson, Rodney	**John Creasey**
Maurois, André	**Emile Salomon Wilhelm Herzog**
Maynwaring, Archibald	**H(oward) P(hillips) Lovecraft**
Meade, Elizabeth Thomasina	**Elizabeth Thomasina Meade Smith**
Meade, L.T.	**Elizabeth Thomasina Meade Smith**
Meek, S.P.	**Sterner St. Paul Meek**
Meek, Sterner St. Paul	*S.P. Meek*
	Sterner St. Paul
Melmoth, Sebastian	**Oscar (Fingal O'Flahertie Wills) Wilde**
Mental Traveller, A	**Edward Alexander Crowley**
Merchant, Paul	**Harlan (Jay) Ellison**
Merlyn, Arthur	**James (Benjamin) Blish**
Merrill, P.J.	**Holly Roth**
Merriman, Alex	**Robert Silverberg**
Merritt, Aimee	**Forrest J(ames) Ackerman**
Metcalf, Suzanne	**L(yman) Frank Baum**
Meyer, Gustav	*Gustav Meyrink*
Meyrink, Gustav	**Gustav Meyer**
Michaelson, John Nairne	**Maxwell Anderson**
Miles	**Edward Alexander Crowley**
	Stephen Southwold
Militant	**Carl A. Sandburg**
Millar, Kenneth	*John Macdonald*
	John Ross Macdonald
	Ross Macdonald
Millay, Edna St. Vincent	*Edna St. Vincent Millay Boissevain*
	Nancy Boyd
Miller, Cincinnatus Heine	*Joaquin Miller*
Miller, Henry	*Phineas Flapdoodle*
Miller, Joaquin	**Cincinnatus Heine Miller**
Mills, S.J.	**Edward Alexander Crowley**
Mitchell, Clyde	**Harlan (Jay) Ellison and Robert Silverberg**
Mitchell, Clyde (T.)	**(Gordon) Randall (Phillip David) Garrett**
Mitchell, Donald G(rant)	*Ik Marvel*
Mohammed	**Edward Alexander Crowley**
Mondelle, Wendayne	**Forrest J(ames) Ackerman**
Moorcock, Michael (John)	*Bill Barclay*
	William Ewert Barclay
	Michael Barrington
	E(dward) P. Bradbury
	James Colvin
	Philip James
	Hank Janson
	Desmond Reid
Moore, C(atherine) L(ucille)	*Keith Hammond*
	Hudson Hastings
	C.H. Liddell
	Mrs. Henry Kuttner
	C.L. Moore
	Lawrence O'Donnell
	Lewis Padgett

Morck, Paal	O(le) E(dvart) Rølvaag
Morgan, Jane	James Fenimore Cooper
Morgenstern, S.	William Goldman
Morland, Peter Henry	Frederick Schiller Faust
Morley, Brian	Marion Zimmer Bradley
Morley, Wilfred Owen	Robert (Augustine) W(ard) Lowndes
Morpheus	Edward Alexander Crowley
Morrison, Richard	Robert (Augustine) W(ard) Lowndes
Morrison, Robert	Robert (Augustine) W(ard) Lowndes
Morrison, Toni	Chloe Anthony Wofford
Morton, Anthony	John Creasey
Mourner Clad In Green, A	Edward Alexander Crowley
Muddock, James Edward	*Dick Donovan*
	Joyce E(mmerson) Preston-Muddock
Mude, O.	Edward (St. John) Gorey
Multatuli	Eduard Douwes Dekker
Mulvey, Thomas	*Victor W. Appleton II*
Munchausen, Baron	Hugo Gernsback
Mundy, Talbot	William L(ancaster) Gribbon
Munro, H(ector) H(ugh)	*Saki*
Munroe, Duncan H.	Eric F(rank) Russell
Murgatroyd, Matthew	James Athearn Jones
Myles, Simon	Ken(neth Martin) Follett
Nabokov, Vladimir Dmitrievich	*V. Nabokov-Sirin*
	V. Sirin
Nabokov-Sirin, V.	Vladimir Dmitrievich Nabokov
Natale, Francine de	Barry N. Malzberg
Nathan, Daniel	Frederic Dannay
Nesbit, E.	E(dith Nesbit) Bland
New England minister	Edward Everett Hale
Newlands, Percy W., P.R.A.S., P.H.B.S...	Edward Alexander Crowley
New York Specialist, A	Edward Alexander Crowley
Nichols, Leigh	Dean (Ray) Koontz
Norden, Charles	Lawrence (George) Durrell
Norfolk, Hilda	Edward Alexander Crowley
Norfolk, William	Philip José Farmer
North, Andrew	Alice Mary Norton
North, Anthony	Dean (Ray) Koontz
Grace May North	Carol Norton
Northrop, Capt. B.A	L(a Fayette) Ron(ald) Hubbard Sr.
Norton, Andre	Alice Mary Norton
Norton, Carol	*Grace May North*
Norvil, Manning	(Henry) Kenneth Bulmer
Norway, Nevil Shute	*Nevil Shute*
Nosille, Nalrah	Harlan (Jay) Ellison
Novak, Joseph	Jerzy (Nikodem) Kosinski
Nye, Bill	Egar Wilson Nye
Nye, Egar Wilson	*Bill Nye*
O., E.G.	Edward Alexander Crowley
Oates, Joyce Carol	*Fernandes*
	Joyce Carol Oates Smith
	Rosamond Smith
O'Brien, Dean D.	Earl Andrew Binder and Otto O(scar) Binder
O'Brien, Dee	Marion Zimmer Bradley
O'Brien, E.G.	Arthur C(harles) Clarke
O'Donnell, K.M., Jr.	Barry N(orman) Malzberg
O'Donnell, Lawrence	C(yril) M. Kornbluth, Henry Kuttner
	and C(atherine) L(ucille) Moore
O'Donovan, Finn	Robert Sheckley
Ogden, H.B.	Isaac Asimov
Ogilvy, Gavin	J.M. Barrie

O'Hara, Scott	**John D(ann) MacDonald**
O. Henry	**William Sydney Porter**
Oldmann, Jeffries	**Algirdas Jonas Budrys**
Oldstyle, Jonathan	**Washington Irving**
Oliver, Chad	**Symmes Chadwick Oliver**
Oliver, Frederick S.	*Phylos the Tibetan*
Oliver, George	*Oliver Onions*
Oliver, Symmes Chadwick	*Chad Oliver*
Omega	**Ray(mond Douglas) Bradbury**
Onions, Oliver	**George Oliver**
Optic, Oliver	**William Taylor Adams**
Orczy, Baroness	**Mrs. Montague Barstow**
Orczy, Emma Magdalena Rosalia Maria Josefa Barbara	**Mrs. Montague Barstow**
O'Reilly, John	*Tex O'Reilly*
O'Reilly, Tex	**John O'Reilly**
Orson, Richard	*Frances & Richard Lockeridge*
Orwell, George	**Eric Arthur Blair**
Osborne, David	**Robert Silverberg**
Osborne, George	**Robert Silverberg**
Osceola	**Karen Christence Blixen-Finecke**
Otis, James	**James Otis Kaler**
Ouida	**(Marie) Louise de la Ramée**
Oursler, (Charles) Fulton	*Anthony Abbott*
	Arnold Fountain
	Samri Frikell
Ouspensky, P.D.	**Petr Uspenskii**
Oz, Amos	**Amos Klausner**
Padgett, Lewis	**Henry Kuttner and C(atherine) L(ucille) Moore**
Page, Jake	**James Keena Page Jr.**
Page, James Keena, Jr.	*Jake Page*
Paget-Lowe, H(enry)	**H(oward) P(hillips) Lovecraft**
Paige, Richard	**Dean (Ray) Koontz**
Paley, Morton D.	**Sam(uel Kimball) Merwin Jr.**
Pansy	**Isabella MacDonald Alden**
Panurge	**Edward Alexander Crowley**
Park, Jordan	**C(yril) M. Kornbluth and Frederik (George) Pohl**
Park, Robert	**Erle Stanley Gardner**
Parker, Bert	**Harlan (Jay) Ellison**
Parker, Dorothy	**Dorothy Rothschild**
Parker, Leslie	**Angela (MacKail) Thirkell**
Parker, Lucas	**John Wyndham Parkes Lucas Beynon Harris**
Parkes, Lucas	**John Wyndham Parkes Lucas Beynon Harris**
Parkes, Wyndham	**John Wyndham Parkes Lucas Beynon Harris**
Parnell, Francis	**Festus Pragnell**
Parr, Robert	**Erle Stanley Gardner**
Parsons, Enid, aged twelve	**Edward Alexander Crowley**
Paul, Sterner St.	**S.P. Meek**
Pearson, Martin	**C(yril) M. Kornbluth and Donald A(llen) Wollheim**
Pellume, Noam D.	**Orson Scott Card**
Pendennis, Arthur	**William Makepeace Thackeray**
Pendleton, Don	**Chet Cunningham**
Pendleton, Don(ald Eugene)	*Dan Britain*
	Stephan Gregory
Pentecost, Hugh	**Judson (Pentecost) Phillips**
Percurabo	**Edward Alexander Crowley**
Perdurabo	**Edward Alexander Crowley**
Perdurabo, Frater	**Edward Alexander Crowley**
Perdurabo, Prater	**Edward Alexander Crowley**
Perez, Juan	**Manly Wade Wellman**
Perse, St. John	**Aléxis St. Léger**
Person of Honour, A	**Jonathan Swift**

Person of Quality, A	**Jonathan Swift**
Peshkov, Alexi Maximovitch	*Maxim Gorki*
Petaja, Emil (Theodore)	*Theodore Pine*
Peters, Curtis Arnoux	*Peter Arno*
Pfaal, Hans	**Edgar Allan Poe**
Philips, Hugh Pentecost	**Judson Philips**
Philips, Judson	*Hugh Pentecost Philips*
Phillips, James Atlee	*Philip Atlee*
Phillips, Judson (Pentecost)	*Phillips, Mark*
Phillips, Richard	**Philip K(indred) Dick**
Phylos the Tibetan	**Frederick S. Oliver**
Phypps, Hyacinthe	**Edward (St. John) Gorey**
Pig, Edward	**Edward (St. John) Gorey**
Pike, Robert L.	**Robert L(loyd) Fish**
Pitcairn, J(ohn) J(ames)	*Clifford Ashdown*
Plath, Sylvia	*Sylvia Hughes*
	Victoria Lucas
Platts, A. Monmouth	**A(nthony) B(erkeley) Cox**
Plick et Plock	**Georges Simenon**
Plunkett, Edward John Moreton Drax	*Lord Dunsany*
Poe, Edgar Allan	*Hans Pfaal*
	Quarles
Pohl, Frederik (George), (Jr.)	*Elton V. Andrews*
	Henry De Costa
	Paul Flehr
	S.D. Gottesman
	Warren F. Howard
	Walt Lasly
	Paul Dennis Lavond
	James MacCreigh
	Scott Mariner
	Ernest Mason
	Ernst Mason
	Edson McCann
	Jordan Park
	Charles Satterfield
	Dirk Wylie
	Allen Zweig
Porter, William Sydney	*O. Henry*
Poum et Zette	**Georges Simenon**
Pound, Ezra (Weston Loomis)	*Alfred Venison*
Power, Cecil	**Charles Grant Blairfindie Allen**
Pragnell, Festus	*Francis Parnell*
Prather, Richard S(cott)	*David Knight*
	Douglas Ring
Pratt, Dennis	*Quentin Crisp*
Pratt, (Murray) Fletcher	*George U. Fletcher*
	Irwin Lester
	B.F. Ruby
Prescot, Dray	**(Henry) Kenneth Bulmer**
Prescot, J.	**(Henry) Kenneth Bulmer**
Probationer	**Edward Alexander Crowley**
Prometheus	**Edward Alexander Crowley**
Pronzini, Bill	**William John Pronzini**
Pronzini, William John	*Robert Hart Davis*
	Jack Foxx
	Brett Halliday
	William Jeffrey
	Bill Pronzini
	Alex Saxon
	Jack Saxon

Prospero and Caliban	**Frederick William Rolfe**
Pryor, Vanessa	**Chelsea Quinn Yarbro**
Pudor, Prob	**Edward Alexander Crowley**
Putnam, Arthur Lee	**Horatio Alger**
Putnam, J. Wesley	**Harry Sinclair Drago**
Puzo, Mario	*Mario Cleri*
Pyeshkov, Aleksei Maksimovich	*Maxim Gorki [Gorky]*
Q	**Arthur T(homas) Quiller-Couch**
Quarles	**Edgar Allan Poe**
Queen, Ellery	**Frederic Dannay** and **Manfred Bennington Lepovsky**
Quiller, A., Jr.	**Edward Alexander Crowley**
Quiller, Andrew	**(Henry) Kenneth Bulmer**
Quiller-Couch, Arthur T(homas)	*Q*
Quinn, Martin	**Martin Cruz Smith**
Quinn, Simon	**Martin Cruz Smith**
Quyth, Gabriel	**Gary Jennings**
R., C.G.	**Christina G(eorgina) Rossetti**
Rabelais, François	*Alcofribas Nasier*
Rabinowitz, Sholem Yakov	*Sholem Aleichem*
Rachen, Kurt Von	**L(a Fayette) Ron(ald) Hubbard**
Raine, William MacLeod	*Austin MacLeod*
Raleigh, Richard	**H(oward) P(hillips) Lovecraft**
Ramsay, Ethel	**Edward Alexander Crowley**
Ramsay, Jay	**(John) Ramsey Campbell**
Rand, Ayn	**Alisa Rosenbaum**
Randall, Robert	**(Gordon) Randall (Phillip David) Garrett** and **Robert Silverberg**
Ranger, Ken	**John Creasey**
Rawlins, Eustace	**Eustace Robert Barton**
Rayner, Olive Pratt	**Charles Grant Blairfindie Allen**
Reader, Constant	**Dorothy Rothschild**
Reed, Eliot	**Eric Ambler** and **Charles Rodda**
Reed, Ishmael	*Emmett Coleman*
Reed, Peter	**John D(ann) MacDonald**
Reilly, William K.	**John Creasey**
Reizenstein, Elmer L(eopold)	*Elmer (L.) Rice*
Remus, Uncle	**Joel Chandler Harris**
Rendell, Ruth	*Barbara Vine*
Repp, Ed(ward) Earl	*John Cody*
	Peter Field
Reynolds, Ron	**Ray(mond Douglas) Bradbury**
Rice, Elmer (L.)	**Elmer L(eopold) Reizenstein**
Richards, Fra	**Robert (Ranke) Graves** and **Charles (Harold St. John) Hamilton**
Ridgway, Jason	**Milton Lesser**
Riley, James Whitcomb	*Benj(amin) F. Johnson*
Riley, Tex	**John Creasey**
Roberts, John	**David Ernest Bingley**
	Edward Alexander Crowley
Roberts, Kenneth	**Lester Dent**
Roberts, Lawrence	**Robert L(loyd) Fish**
Roberts, Terence	**Ivan T. Sanderson**
Robertson, Constance (Pierrepont) Noyes	*Dana Scott*
Robertson, Ellis	**Harlan (Jay) Ellison** and **Robert Silverberg**
Rodman, Eric	**Robert Silverberg**
Roeder, Pat	**Harlan (Jay) Ellison**
Rogers, Doug	**Ray(mond Douglas) Bradbury**
Rohmer, Sax	**Arthur (Henry) Sarsfield Ward**
Rolfe, Frederick William	*Baron (Frederick) Corvo*
	Prospero and Caliban
Rølvaag, O(le) E(dvart)	*Paal Morck*
Romaine, Jules	**Louis Fairigoule**
Romanoff, Alexander Nicholayevitch	*Achmed Abdullah*

	Chrisophe des Laurieres
Smith, Doc	**E(dward) E(lmer) "Doc" Smith**
Smith, E(dward) E(lmer) "Doc"	*Doc Smith*
Smith, Elizabeth Thomasina Meade	*Elizabeth Thomasina Meade*
	L.T. Meade
Smith, Ernest Bramah	*Ernest Bramah*
Smith, Johnston	**Stephen Crane**
Smith, Joyce Carol Oates	**Joyce Carol Oates**
Smith, Kate Douglas	*Kate Douglas Wiggin*
Smith, Rosamond	**Joyce Carol Oates**
Smith, T. Carlyle	**John Kendrick Bangs**
Smith, Woodrow Wilson	**Henry Kuttner**
Snell, Roy. J.	*James Craig*
Softly, Edward	**H(oward) P(hillips) Lovecraft**
Solo, Jay	**Harlan (Jay) Ellison**
Somers, Jane	**Doris (May) Lessing**
Somers, Jonathan Swift, III	**Philip José Farmer**
Southern, Terry	*Maxwell Kenton*
Sparks, Timothy	**Charles Dickens**
Spaulding, Douglas	**Ray(mond Douglas) Bradbury**
Spaulding, Leonard	**Ray(mond Douglas) Bradbury**
Spencer, John	**Roy (C.) Vickers**
Spencer, Leonard G(**Gordon) Randall (Phillip David) Garrett** & **Robert Silverberg**
Stairs, Gordon	**Mary H(unter) Austin**
Stanislavsky, Constantin	**Constantin Sergeyevich Alekseyev**
Stanton, Schuyler	**L(yman) Frank Baum**
Stark, Richard	**D(onald) E(dwin) Westlake**
Starr, Julian	**Horatio Alger**
Staunton, Schuyler	**L(yman) Frank Baum**
Steele, Addison E.	**Richard A(llen) Lupoff**
Stendahl	**Marie-Henri Beyle**
Stendahl, Baron de	**Marie-Henri Beyle**
Steptoe, Lydia	**Djuna Barnes**
Sterling, Brett	**Ray(mond Douglas) Bradbury** and **Edmond (Moore) Hamilton**
Stewart, J(ohn) I(nnes) M(ackintosh)	*Michael Innes*
St. John, David	**E(verette) Howard Hunt Jr.**
St. John, Henry	**John Creasey**
St. John, John	**Edward Alexander Crowley**
Stoddard, Charles	**Henry Kuttner**
Stone, I.F.	**Isidor Feinstein**
Stone, Irving	*Irving Tannenbaum*
Stowe, Harriet Beecher	**Harriet (Elizabeth) Beecher**
Sturgeon, Theodore	**Edward Hamilton Waldo**
Svaroff, Count Vladimir	**Edward Alexander Crowley**
Swift, Jonathan	*Isaac Bickerstaff*
	A Dissenter
	M.B. Drapier
	A Person of Honour
	A Person of Quality
	T.R.D.J.S.D.O.P.I.I.]
Swithen, John	**Stephen (Edwin) King**
Sydney, Margaret	**Harriet M. Lothrop**
T., H.K.	**Edward Alexander Crowley**
T., J.	**Eric Temple Bell**
Tabasco, Alexander	**Edward Alexander Crowley**
Taine, John	**Eric Temple Bell**
Tait, Eric	**Edward Alexander Crowley**
Tannenbaum, Irving	**Irving Stone**
Tanner, William	**(Sir) Kingsley (William) Amis**
Tarr, M.S.	**Edward Alexander Crowley**
Tarrant, John	**Clive Egleton**

Taylor, Phoebe Atwood	*Alice Tilton*
T.B.A.	**Thomas Bailey Aldrich**
Tenn, William	**Philip (J.) Klass**
Terry, C.V.	**Frank G(ill) Slaughter**
Thackeray, William Makepeace	*Arthur Pendennis*
	Michael Angelo Titmarsh
	Theophile Wagstaff]
Thelema, Logos Aionos	**Edward Alexander Crowley**
Theobold, Lewis, Jr.	**H(oward) P(hillips) Lovecraft**
Therion	**Edward Alexander Crowley**
Therion, Master	**Edward Alexander Crowley**
Therion, To Mega DCLXVI	**Edward Alexander Crowley**
Thibault, Jacques-Anatole-François	*Anatole France*
	Gérôme
Thomas, David	**Edward Alexander Crowley**
Thornton, Hall	**Robert Silverberg**
Three, C. Three	**Oscar Wilde**
Tiger, Derry	**Harlan (Jay) Ellison**
Torquemada	**John Dickson Carr**
Torr, Alice Wesley	**Edward Alexander Crowley**
Tourgée, Albion W(inegar)	*Henry Churton*
	Edgar Henry
Traven, B.	**Berick Traven Torsvan**
T.R.D.J.S.D.O.P.I.I.	**Jonathan Swift**
Trevor, Glen	**James Hilton**
Trueblood, Ernest V.	**William (Cuthbert) Faulkner**
Tupper, M.	**Edward Alexander Crowley**
Turner, J.	**Edward Alexander Crowley**
Twain, Mark	**Samuel Langhorne Clemens**
Undercliffe, Errol	**(John) Ramsey Campbell**
Uriel, Henry	**Frederick Schiller Faust**
Uspenskii, Petr	*P.D. Ouspensky*
Vace, Geoffrey	**Hugh B. Cave**
Vadé, Catherine	**François Marie Arouet**
Vadé, Guillaume	**François Marie Arouet**
Van Campen, Karl	**John Wood Campbell Jr.**
Van Dine, S.S.	**Willard Huntington Wright**
Van Dyne, Edith	**L(yman) Frank Baum**
Vardeman, Robert (Bob) E(dward)	*Victor W. Appleton II*
	Paul Kenyon,
	Daniel Moran
Vedder, John K.	**Frank Gruber**
Verey, Rev C.	**Edward Alexander Crowley**
Vernon, Olivia	**Anne Brontë**
Vialis, Gaston	**Georges Simenon**
Vialo, G.	**Georges Simenon**
Viaud, L.M. Julien	*Pierre Loti*
Vicarion, Count Palmiro	**Christopher Logue**
Victor	**Edward Alexander Crowley**
Vidal, Eugene Luther Gore, Jr.	*Edgar Box*
Viffa, Ananda	**Edward Alexander Crowley**
Vigil	**Arthur Koestler**
Vijja, Ananda	**Edward Alexander Crowley**
Vincey, Leo	**Edward Alexander Crowley**
Vine, Barbara	**Ruth Rendell**
Violis, G.	**Georges Simenon**
Viridis, Leo	**Edward Alexander Crowley**
Voltaire	**François Marie Arouet**
Von Drey, Howard	**Howard E(lmer) Wandrei**
von Rachen, Kurt	**L(a Fayette) Ron(ald) Hubbard Sr.**
Von Schartzkopf, Professor Theophilus, Ph.D,	**Edward Alexander Crowley**

Reasons to Collect

Like if you bought this book you needed one. It's a book after all, it was meant to be collected somewhere by someone or something, and the reasons for that are too numerous to catalouge. I know a collector who collects books with angels on the cover. In fact he has paid me rather well, at times, to find books with angels on the cover. Collecting prize-winning books or authors is, at best, a tiny plurality among book collectors. I suspect because they want to hide their insanity behind a facade of normality, and actually build a facade over their mania that reveals to the whole world a science and methodolgy to cloak their insanity. Either that or they actually believe that the self-serving, self-promoting politics of book prizes has some deep metphysical meaning. Which is a great deal of self-delusionary fun so I included this section.

Winners of the Nobel Prize in Literature

2008 - Jean-Marie Gustave Le Clézio
2007 - Doris Lessing
2006 - Orhan Pamuk
2005 - Harold Pinter
2004 - Elfriede Jelinek
2003 - J. M. Coetzee
2002 - Imre Kertész
2001 - V. S. Naipaul
2000 - Gao Xingjian
1999 - Günter Grass
1998 - José Saramago
1997 - Dario Fo
1996 - Wislawa Szymborska
1995 - Seamus Heaney
1994 - Kenzaburo Oe
1993 - Toni Morrison
1992 - Derek Walcott
1991 - Nadine Gordimer
1990 - Octavio Paz
1989 - Camilo José Cela
1988 - Naguib Mahfouz
1987 - Joseph Brodsky
1986 - Wole Soyinka
1985 - Claude Simon
1984 - Jaroslav Seifert
1983 - William Golding
1982 - Gabriel García Márquez
1981 - Elias Canetti
1980 - Czeslaw Milosz
1979 - Odysseus Elytis
1978 - Isaac Bashevis Singer
1977 - Vicente Aleixandre
1976 - Saul Bellow
1975 - Eugenio Montale
1974 - Eyvind Johnson, Harry Martinson
1973 - Patrick White
1972 - Heinrich Böll
1971 - Pablo Neruda

1954 - Ernest Hemingway
1953 - Winston Churchill
1952 - François Mauriac
1948 - T.S. Eliot
1947 - André Gide
1946 - Hermann Hesse
1945 - Gabriela Mistral
1944 - Johannes V. Jensen
1943 - None
1942 - None
1941 - None
1940 - None
1939 - Frans Eemil Sillanpää
1938 - Pearl Buck
1937 - Roger Martin du Gard
1936 - Eugene O'Neill
1935 - None
1934 - Luigi Pirandello
1933 - Ivan Bunin
1932 - John Galsworthy
1931 - Erik Axel Karlfeldt
1930 - Sinclair Lewis
1929 - Thomas Mann
1928 - Sigrid Undset
1927 - Henri Bergson
1926 - Grazia Deledda
1925 - George Bernard Shaw
1924 - Wladyslaw Reymont
1923 - William Butler Yeats
1922 - Jacinto Benavente
1921 - Anatole France
1920 - Knut Hamsun
1919 - Carl Spitteler
1918 - None
1917 - Karl Gjellerup, Henrik Pontoppidan
1916 - Verner von Heidenstam
1915 - Romain Rolland
1914 - None

1970 - Alexandr Solzhenitsyn
1969 - Samuel Beckett
1968 - Yasunari Kawabata
1967 - Miguel Angel Asturias
1966 - Shmuel Agnon, Nelly Sachs
1965 - Mikhail Sholokhov
1964 - Jean-Paul Sartre
1963 - Giorgos Seferis
1962 - John Steinbeck
1961 - Ivo Andric
1960 - Saint-John Perse
1959 - Salvatore Quasimodo
1958 - Boris Pasternak
1957 - Albert Camus
1956 - Juan Ramón Jiménez
1955 - Halldór Laxness

1913 - Rabindranath Tagore
1912 - Gerhart Hauptmann
1911 - Maurice Maeterlinck
1910 - Paul Heyse
1909 - Selma Lagerlöf
1908 - Rudolf Eucken
1907 - Rudyard Kipling
1906 - Giosuè Carducci
1905 - Henryk Sienkiewicz
1904 - Frédéric Mistral, José Echegaray
1903 - Bjørnstjerne Bjørnson
1902 - Theodor Mommsen
1901 - Sully Prudhomme

Pulitzer Prize Winners
Biography and Autobiography

2009 - Jon Meacham. **American Lion: Andrew Jackson in the White House.** NY: Random House, 2008.

2008 - John Matteson. **Eden's Outcasts: The Story of Louisa May Alcott and Her Father.** NY: W.W. Norton, 2007.

2007 - Debby Applegate. **The Most Famous Man in America: The Biography of Henry Ward Beecher.** Garden City, NY: Doubleday, 2006.

2006- Kai Bird and Martin J. Sherwin. **American Prometheus: The Triumph and Tragedy of J. Robert Oppenheimer.** Westminister, MD: Alfred A. Knopf, 2005.

2005- Mark Stevens and Annalyn Swan. **de Kooning: An American Master** NY: Alfred A. Knopf, 2004.

2004- William Taubman. **Khrushchev: The Man and His Era** NY: W.W. Norton, 2003.

2003- Robert A. Caro. **Master of the Senate.** Westminister, MD: Alfred A. Knopf, 2002.

2002- David McCullough. **John Adams.** NY: Simon & Schuster, 2001.

2001- David Levering Lewis. **W.E.B. Du Bois: The Fight for Equality and the American Century, 1919-1963.** NY: Henry Holt and Company, 2000.

2000- Stacy Schiff. **Vera (Mrs. Vladimir Nabokov).** NY: Random House, 1999.

1999- A. Scott Berg. **Lindbergh.** New York: G. P. Putnam's Sons, 1998.

1998- Katharine Graham. **Personal History.** NY: Alfred A. Knopf, 1997.

1997- Frank McCourt. **Angela's Ashes: A Memoir.** NY: Scribner, 1996.

1996- Jack Miles. **God: A Biography.** Westminister, MD: Alfred A. Knopf, 1995.

1995- Joan D. Hedrick. **Harriet Beecher Stowe: A Life.** Cary, North Carolina: Oxford Univ Pr, 1994

1994- David Levering Lewis. **W.E.B. Du Bois: Biography of a Race 1868-1919.** NY: Henry Holt, 1993.

1993- David McCullough. **Truman.** Riverside, NJ: Simon & Schuster, 1992.

1992- Lewis B. Puller. **Fortunate Son: The Healing of a Vietnam Vet**. NY: Grove Weidenfeld, 1991

1991- Steven Naifeh and Gregory White Smith. **Jackson Pollock.** NY: Clarkson Potter, 1989.

1990- Sebastian de Grazia. **Machiavelli in Hell.** Princeton, NJ: Princeton University Press, 1989.

1989- Richard Ellmann. **Oscar Wilde.** New York: Alfred A. Knopf, 1988.

1988 - David Herbert Donald. **Look Homeward: A Life of Thomas Wolfe.** Boston: Little Brown & Co, 1987.

1987- David J. Garrow. **Bearing the Cross: Martin Luther King Jr. and the Southern Christian Leadership Conference**. New York: William Morrow and Company, 1986.

1986- Elizabeth Frank. **Louise Bogan: A Portrait**. New York: Alfred A. Knopf, 1985.

1985- Kenneth Silverman **The Life and Times of Cotton Mather.** NY: Harper & Row, 1983.

1984- Louis R. Harlan. **Booker T. Washington: The Wizard of Tuskegee, 1901-1915**. New York:,Oxford University Press,1983

1983- Russell Baker. **Growing Up.** New York: Congdon & Weed. 1982

1982- William McFeely. **Grant: A Biography**. New York: Norton, 1981.

1981- Robert K. Massie. **Peter the Great: His Life and World.** New York: Alfred A. Knopf, 1980.

1980- Edmund Morris. **The Rise of Theodore Roosevelt.** NY: Coward, McCann, & Geoghegan, 1979.

1979- Leonard Baker. **Days of Sorrow and Pain: Leo Baeck and the Berlin Jews.** Old Tappan, NJ: Macmillan, 1978.

1978- Walter Jackson Bate. **Samuel Johnson.** New York: Harcourt Brace Jovanovich, 1977.

1977- John E. Mack. **A Prince of Our Disorder: The Life of T. E. Lawrence.** Boston: Little Brown, 1976.

1976- R. W. B. Lewis. **Edith Wharton: A Biography.** New York: Harper & Row, 1975.

1975- Robert Caro. **The Power Broker: Robert Moses and the Fall of New York**. NY: Alfred A. Knopf, 1974.

1974- Louis Sheaffer. **O'Neill, Son and Artist.** Boston: Little, Brown,1973.

1973- W. A. Swanberg. **Luce and His Empire.** New York: Scribner, 1972.

1972- Joseph P. Lash. **Eleanor and Franklin.** NY: W W Norton & Co Inc, 1971.

1971- Lawrence Thompson. **Robert Frost: The Years of Triumph, 1915 -1938.** NY: Henry Holt, 1970.

1970- T. Harry Williams. **Huey Long**. New York: Alfred A. Knopf, 1969.

1969- Benjamin Lawrence Reid. **The Man From New York: John Quinn and His Friends.** New York: Oxford University Press, 1968.
1968 - George F. Kennan. **Memoirs.** Boston: Little, Brown, 1967.
1967 - Justin Kaplan. **Mr. Clemens and Mark Twain**. New York: Simon and Schuster, 1966.
1966- Arthur M. Schlesinger. **A Thousand Days.** Boston: Houghton Mifflin, 1965.
1965- Ernest Samuels. **Henry Adams.** Cambridge, MA: Belknap Press of Harvard University, 1965. (Three Volumes)
1964- Walter Jackson Bate. **John Keats** Cambridge, MA: Belknap Press of Harvard University, 1963.
1963- Leon Edel. **Henry James.** Philadelphia: Lippincott, 1962.
1962 (No Award)
1961- David Donald. **Charles Sumner and the Coming of the Civil War.** NY: Alfred A. Knopf, 1960.
1960- Samuel Eliot Morison. **John Paul Jones**. Boston: Little, Brown, 1959.
1959- Arthur Walworth. **Woodrow Wilson, American Prophet.** NY: Longmans, Green and Co., 1958.
1958- Douglas Southall Freeman. **George Washington, Volumes I-VI.** New York: Scribner's. 1948-57.
1957- John F. Kennedy. **Profiles in Courage.** NY: Harper's, 1955.
1956- Talbot Faulkner Hamlin. **Benjamin Henry Latrobe.** New York, Oxford University Press, 1955.
1955- William S. White. **The Taft Story.** NY: Harper & Bros, 1954.
1954- Charles A. Lindbergh. **The Spirit of St. Louis.** New York: Scribner's, 1953.
1953- David J. Mays. **Edmund Pendleton 1721-1803.** Cambridge, MA: Harvard University Press, 1952.
1952- Merlo J. Pusey. **Charles Evans Hughes.** New York: Macmillan, 1951.
1951- Margaret Louise Coit. **John C. Calhoun: American Portrait.** Boston: Houghton Mifflin, 1950.
1950- Samuel Flagg Bemis. **John Quincy Adams and the Foundations of American Foreign Policy.** New York: Alfred A. Knopf, 1949.
1949- Robert E. Sherwood. **Roosevelt and Hopkins**. New York: Harper, 1948.
1948- Margaret Clapp. **Forgotten First Citizen: John Bigelow.** Boston: Little Brown, 1947.
1947- William Allen White. **The Autobiography of William Allen White.** New York: Macmillan, 1946.
1946- Linnie Marsh Wolfe. **Son of the Wilderness.** New York: Alfred A. Knopf, 1945.
1945- Russell Blaine Nye. **George Bancroft: Brahmin Rebel.** New York: Alfred A. Knopf, 1944.

1944- Carleton Mabee. **The American Leonardo: The Life of Samuel F B. Morse.** New York: Alfred A. Knopf, 1943.

1943- Samuel Eliot Morison. **Admiral of the Ocean Sea.** Boston: Little Brown, 1942.

1942- Forrest Wilson. **Crusader in Crinoline.** Philadelphia: J.B. Lippincott Company, 1941.

1941- Ola Elizabeth Winslow. **Jonathan Edward.** New York: Macmillan, 1940.

1940- Ray Stannard Baker. **Woodrow Wilson, Life and Letters. Vols. VII and VIII.** Garden City, NY: Doubleday, 1939.

1939- Carl Van Doren. **Benjamin Franklin.** New York: The Viking Press, 1938.

1938- Marquis James. **Andrew Jackson.** Indianapolis: Bobbs-Merrill, 1937.

1938- Odell Shepard. **Pedlar's Progress.** Boston: Little Brown, 1937.

1937- Allan Nevins. **Hamilton Fish.** New York, Dodd, Mead, 1936.

1936- Ralph Barton Perry. **The Thought and Character of William James.** Boston: Little Brown, 1935.

1935- Douglas S. Freeman. **R. E. Lee.** New York: Scribner's, 1934.

1934- Tyler Dennett. **John Hay.** New York, Dodd, Mead, 1933.

1933- Allan Nevins. **Grover Cleveland.** New York, Dodd, Mead, 1932.

1932- Henry F. Pringle. *Theodore Roosevelt* NY: Harcourt, 1931.

1931- Henry James. **Charles W. Eliot.** Boston: Houghton Mifflin, 1930.

1930- Marquis James. **The Raven.** Indianapolis: Bobbs-Merrill, 1929.

1929- Burton J. Hendrick. The **Training of an American: The Earlier Life and Letters of Walter H. Page.** Boston: Houghton Mifflin, 1928.

1928- Charles Edward Russell. **The American Orchestra and Theodore Thomas.** Garden City, NY: Doubleday, 1927.

1927- Emory Holloway. **Whitman.** New York: Alfred A. Knopf, 1926.

1926- Harvey Cushing. **The Life of Sir William Osler.** New York: Oxford University Press,1925.

1925- M. A. Dewolfe Howe. **Barrett Wendell and His Letters.** Boston: Little Brown, 1924.

1924- Michael Idvorsky Pupin. **From Immigrant to Inventor.** New York: Scribner's, 1923.

1923- Burton J. Hendrick. **The Life and Letters of Walter H. Page.** Boston: Houghton Mifflin, 1922.

1922- Hamlin Garland. A **Daughter of the Middle Border.** New York: Macmillan, 1921.

1921- Edward Bok. **The Americanization of Edward Bok.** New York: Scribner's, 1920.

1920- Albert J. Beveridge. **The Life of John Marshall.** Boston: Houghton Mifflin, 1919.

1919- Henry Adams. **The Education of Henry Adams.** Boston: Houghton Mifflin, 1918.

1918- William Cabell Bruce. **Benjamin Franklin, Self-Revealed.** NY: Putnam's, 1917.

1917- Laura E. Richards and Maude Howe Elliott assisted by Florence Howe Hall. **Julia Ward Howe.** Boston: Houghton Mifflin, 1915.

Fiction and Novels

2008- Junot Diaz. **The Brief Wonderous Life of Oscar Wao.** NY: Riverhead, 2007.

2007- Cormac McCarthy. **The Road.** NY: Knopf, 2006.

2006- Geraldine Brooks. **March.** NY: Viking, 2005.

2005- Marilynne Robinson. **Gilead.** NY: Farrar, Strauss and Giroux, 2004.

2004- Edward P. Jones. **The Known World.** NY: Amistad, 2003.

2003- Jeffrey Eugenides. **Middlesex.** NY: Farrar, Strauss and Giroux, 2002.

2002- Richard Russo. **Empire Falls.** NY: Knopf, 2001.

2001- Michael Chabon. **The Amazing Adventures of Kavalier and Clay.** NY: Random House, 2000.

2000- Jhumpa Lahiri. **Interpreter of Maladies.** Boston: Houghton Mifflin, 1999.

1999- Michael Cunningham. **The Hours.** NY: Farrar, Strauss and Giroux, 1998.

1998- Philip Roth. **American Pastoral.** Franklin Center, PA: Franklin Library, 1997.

1997- Steven Millhauser. **Martin Dressler: The Tale of an American Dreamer.** NY: Crown, 1996.

1996- Richard Ford. **Independence Day.** NY: Knopf, 1995.

1995- Carol Shields. **The Stone Diaries.** Mississauga, ON, Canada: Random House of Canada, Limited, 1993.

1994- E. Annie Proulx. **The Shipping News.** NY: Scribner, 1993.

1993- Robert Olen Butler. **A Good Scent from a Strange Mountain.** NY: Holt, 1992.

1992- Jane Smiley. **A Thousand Acres.** NY: Knopf. 1991.

1991- John Updike. **Rabbit at Rest.** Franklin Center, PA: Franklin Library, 1990.

1990- Oscar Hijuelos. **The mambo kings play songs of love.** NY: Farrar, Strauss and Giroux, 1989.

1989- Anne Tyler. **Breathing Lessons.** Franklin Center, PA: Franklin Library, 1988.

1988- Toni Morrison. **(Beloved.** NY: Knopf 1987.

1987- Peter Taylor. **A Summons to Memphis.** NY: Knopf, 1986.

1986- Larry McMurtry. **Lonesome Dove.** NY: Simon & Schuster, 1985.

1985- Alison Lurie. **Foreign Affairs:** Franklin Center, PA: Franklin Library, 1984.

1984- William Kennedy. **Ironweed.** NY: Viking, 1983.

1983- Alice Walker. **The Color Purple.** NY: Harcourt, 1982.

1982- John Updike. **Rabbit is Rich.** NY: Knopf, 1981.

1981- John Kennedy Toole. **A Confederacy of Dunces.** Baton Rouge: Louisiana State University Press, 1980.

1980- Norman Mailer. **The Executioner's Song.** Boston: Little Brown, 1979.

1979- John Cheever. **The Stories of John Cheever.** NY: Knopf, 1978.

1978- James Alan McPherson. **Elbow Room.** Boston: Little Brown, 1977.

1977 (No Award)

1976- Saul Bellow. **Humboldt's Gift.** NY: Viking, 1975.

1975- Michael Shaara. **The Killer Angels.** NY: MacKay, 1974.

1974 (No Award)

1973- Eudora Welty. **The Optimist's Daughter**. NY: Random House, 1972.

1972- Wallace Stegner. **Angle of Repose.** Garden City, NY: Doubleday, 1971.

1971 (No Award)

1970- Jean Stafford. **Collected Stories.** NY: Farrar, Strauss and Giroux, 1969.

1969- N. Scott Momaday. **House Made of Dawn.** NY: Harper and Row, 1968.

1968- William Styron. **The Confessions of Nat Turner.** NY: Random House, 1967.

1967- Bernard Malamud. **The Fixer**. NY: Farrar, Strauss and Giroux, 1966.

1966- Katherine Anne Porter. **Collected Stories.** NY: Harcourt, 1965.

1965- Shirley Ann Grau. **The Keepers of the House.** NY: Knopf, 1964.

1964 (No Award)

1963- William Faulkner. **The Reivers.** NY: Random House, 1962.

1962- Edwin O'Connor. **The Edge of Sadness.** Boston: Little Brown, 1961.

1961- Harper Lee. **To Kill a Mockingbird**. Philadelphia and New York, Lippincott, 1960.

1960- Allen Drury. **Advise and Consent.** Garden City, NY: Doubleday, 1959.

1959- Robert Lewis Taylor. **The Travels of Jamie Mcpheeters.** Garden City, NY: Doubleday, 1958.

1958- James Agee. **A Death in the Family**. NY: McDowell Obolensky, 1957.

1957 (No Award)

1956- MacKinlay Kantor. **Andersonville.** Cleveland and New York: World Publishing Company, 1955.

1955- William Faulkner. **A Fable**. NY: Random House, 1954.

1954 (No Award)

1953- Ernest Hemingway. **The Old Man and The Sea.** NY: Scribner, 1952.

1952- Herman Wouk. **The Caine Mutiny.** Garden City, NY: Doubleday, 1951.

1951- Conrad Richter. **The Town**. NY: Knopf, 1950.

1950- A. B. Guthrie. **The Way West.** NY: William Sloane, 1949.

1949- James Gould Cozzens. **Guard of Honor.** NY: Harcourt, 1948.

1948- James A. Michener. **Tales of the South Pacific.** NY: Macmillan, 1947.

1947- Robert Penn Warren. **All the King's Men.** NY: Harcourt, 1946.

1946 (No Award)

1945- John Hersey. **A Bell for Adano.** NY: Knopf, 1944.

1944- Martin Flavin. **Journey in the Dark.** NY: Harper's, 1943.

1943- Upton Sinclair. **Dragon's Teeth.** NY: Viking, 1942.

1942- Ellen Glasgow. **In this Our Life.** NY: Harcourt, 1941.

1941 (No Award)

1940- John Steinbeck. **The Grapes of Wrath.** NY: Viking, 1939.

1939- Marjorie Kinnan Rawlings. **The Yearling.** NY: Scribner's, 1938.

1938- John Phillips Marquand. **The Late George Apley.** Boston: Little Brown, 1937.

1937- Margaret Mitchell. **Gone with the Wind.** NY: Macmillan, 1936.

1936- Harold L. Davis. **Honey in the Horn.** NY: Harper, 1935.

1935- Josephine Winslow Johnson. **Now in November.** NY: Simon & Schuster, 1934.

1934- Caroline Miller. **Lamb in his Bosom.** NY: Harper, 1933.

1933- T. S. Stribling. **The Store.** Garden City, NY: Doubleday Doran, 1932.

1932 Pearl S. Buck. **The Good Earth.** NY: John Day, 1931.

1931- Margaret Ayer Barnes. **Years of Grace.** Boston: Houghton Mifflin, 1930.

1930- Oliver Lafarge. **Laughing Boy.** Boston: Houghton Mifflin, 1929.

1929- Julia Peterkin. **Scarlet Sister Mary.** Indianapolis: Bobbs-Merrill, 1928.

1928 Thornton Wilder. **The Bridge of San Luis Rey.** New York: Albert & Charles Boni, 1927.

1927- Louis Bromfield. **Early Autumn.** NY: Stokes, 1926.

1926- Sinclair Lewis. **Arrowsmith.** NY: Harcourt, 1925.

1925- Edna Ferber. **So Big.** Garden City, NY: Doubleday, Page, 1924.

1924- Margaret Wilson. **The Able McLaughlins.** NY: Harper, 1923.

1923- Willa Cather. **One of Ours.** NY: Knopf, 1922.

1922- Booth Tarkington. **Alice Adams.** Garden City, NY: Doubleday, Page, 1921

1921- Edith Wharton. **The Age of Innocence.** NY: D. Appleton, 1920.

1920 (No Award)

1919- Booth Tarkington. **The Magnificent Ambersons.** Garden City, NY: Doubleday, Page, 1918.

1918- Ernest Poole. **His Family.** NY: Macmillan, 1917.

1917 (No Award)

Poetry

2009- W.S. Merwin. **The Shadow of Sirius.** Port Townsend, WA: Copper Canyon Press, 2008.

2008- Robert Hass. **Time and Materials.** NY: Ecco, 2007.

2008- Philip Schultz. **Failure.** New York: Harcourt, 2007.

2007- Natasha Trethewey. **Native Guard.** Wilmington, MA: Houghton Mifflin, 2006.

2006- Claudia Emerson. **Late Wife.** Baton Rouge: Louisiana State University Press, 2005.

2005- Ted Kooser. **Delights & Shadows.** Port Townsend, WA: Copper Canyon Press, 2004.

2004- Franz Wright. **Walking to Martha's Vineyard.** NY: Knopf, 2003.

2003- Paul Muldoon. **Moy Sand and Gravel.** NY: Farrar, Strauss and Giroux, 2002.

2002- Carl Dennis. **Practical Gods.** New York: Penguin, 2001.

2001- Stephen Dunn. **Different Hours.** New York: W.W. Norton & Company, Inc., 2000.

2000- C.K. Williams. **Repair.** NY: Farrar, Strauss and Giroux, 1999.

1999- Mark Strand. **Blizzard of One.** NY: Knopf, 1998.

1998- Charles Wright. **Black Zodiac.** NY: Farrar, Strauss and Giroux, 1997.

1997- Lisel Mueller. **Alive Together: New and Selected Poems.** Baton Rouge: Louisiana State University Press, 1996.

1996- Jorie Graham. **The Dream of the Unified Field.** Hopewell, New Jersey: The Ecco Press, 1995.

1995- Philip Levine. **The Simple Truth.** NY: Knopf, 1994.

1994- Yusef Komunyakaa. **Neon Vernacular: New and Selected Poems.** Hanover, NH: Wesleyan University Press/University Press of New England, 1993.

1993- Louise Gluck. **The Wild Iris.** Hopewell, New Jersey: The Ecco Press, 1992.

1992- James Tate. **Selected Poems.** Hanover, NH: Wesleyan University Press/University Press of New England, 1991.

1991- Mona Van Duyn. **Near Changes.** New York: Alfred A. Knopf, 1990.

1990- Charles Simic. **The World Doesn't End.** NY: Harcourt, 1989.

1989- Richard Wilbur. **New and Collected Poems.** NY: Harcourt, 1988.

1988- William Meredith. **Partial Accounts: New and Selected Poems.** New York: Alfred A. Knopf, 1987.

1987- Rita Dove. **Thomas and Beulah.** Pittsburgh: Carnegie-Mellon University Press, 1986.

1986- Henry Taylor. **The Flying Change.** Baton Rouge: Louisiana State University Press, 1985.

1985- Carolyn Kizer. **Yin.** Brockport, NY: BOA Editions, 1984.

1984- Mary Oliver. **American Primitive.** Boston: Little Brown, 1983.

1983- Galway Kinnell. **Selected Poems.** Boston: Houghton Mifflin, 1982.

1982- Sylvia Plath. **The Collected Poems.** NY: Harper and Row, 1981.

1981- James Schuyler. **The Morning of the Poem.** NY: Farrar, Strauss and Giroux, 1980.

1980 Donald Justice. **Selected Poems.** NY. Atheneum, 1979.

1979- Robert Penn Warren. **Now and Then.** NY: Random House, 1978.

1978- Howard Nemerov. **Collected Poems.** Chicago: University of Chicago Press, 1977.

1977- James Merrill. **Divine Comedies.** NY: Atheneum, 1976.

1976- John Ashbery. **Self-Portrait in a Convex Mirror.** NY: Viking, 1975.

1975- Gary Snyder. **Turtle Island,** NY: New Directions, 1974.

1974- Robert Lowell. **The Dolphin.** NY: Farrar, Strauss and Giroux, 1973.

1973- Maxine Kumin. **Up Country.** NY: Harper and Row, 1972.

1972- James Wright. **Collected Poems.** Middletown, CT: Wesleyan University Press, 1971.

1971- William S. Merwin. **The Carrier of Ladders.** NY: Atheneum, 1970.

1970- Richard Howard. **Untitled Subjects.** NY: Atheneum, 1969.

1969- George Oppen. **Of Being Numerous.** NY: New Directions, 1968.

1968- Anthony Hecht. **The Hard Hours.** NY: Atheneum, 1967.

1967- Anne Sexton. **Live or Die.** Boston: Houghton Mifflin, 1966.

1966- Richard Eberhart. **Selected Poems 1930-1965.** NY: New Directions, 1965.

1965- John Berryman. **77 Dream Songs.** NY: Farrar, Strauss and Giroux, 1964.

1964- Louis Simpson. **At The End Of The Open Road.** Middletown, CT: Wesleyan University Press, 1963.

1963- William Carlos Williams. **Pictures from Brueghel.** Norfolk, CT: New Directions, 1962.

1962- Alan Dugan. **Poems.** New Haven: Yale University Press, 1961.

1961- Phyllis McGinley. **Times Three: Selected Verse From Three Decades.** NY: Viking, 1960.

1960- W. D. Snodgrass. **Heart's Needle.** NY: Knopf, 1959.

1959- Stanley Kunitz. **Selected Poems 1928-1958.** Boston: Little Brown, 1958.

1958- Robert Penn Warren. **Promises: Poems 1954-1956.** NY: Random House, 1957.

1957- Richard Wilbur. **Things of This World.** New York: Harcourt, 1956.

1956- Elizabeth Bishop. **Poems - North & South.** Boston: Houghton Mifflin, 1955.

1955- Wallace Stevens. **Collected Poems.** NY: Knopf, 1954.

1954- Theodore Roethke. **The Waking.** Garden City, NY: Doubleday, 1953.

1953- Archibald MacLeish. **Collected Poems 1917-1952.** Boston: Houghton Mifflin, 1952.

1952- Marianne Moore. **Collected Poems.** New York: Macmillan, 1951.

1951- Carl Sandburg. **Complete Poems.** New York: Harcourt, 1950.

1950- Gwendolyn Brooks. **Annie Allen.** NY: Harper, 1949.

1949- Peter Viereck. **Terror and Decorum.** New York, Charles Scribner's Sons, 1948.

1948- W. H. Auden. **The Age of Anxiety.** NY: Random House, 1947.

1947- Robert Lowell. **Lord Weary's Castle.** New York: Harcourt, 1946.

1946 (No Award)

1945- Karl Shapiro. **V-Letter and Other Poems.** New York: Reynal & Hitchcock, 1944.

1944- Stephen Vincent Benet. **Western Star.** New York/Toronto, Farrar & Rinehart, Inc., 1943.

1943- Robert Frost. **A Witness Tree.** NY: Henry Holt, 1942.

1942- William Rose Benet. **The Dust Which Is God.** NY: Dodd, Mead & Co., 1941.

1941- Leonard Bacon. **Sunderland Capture.** NY: Harper, 1940.

1940- Mark Van Doren. **Collected Poems.** NY: Henry Holt, 1939.

1939- John Gould Fletcher. **Selected Poems.** New York/Toronto, Farrar & Rinehart, Inc., 1938.

1938- Marya Zaturenska. **Cold Morning Sky.** New York: Macmillan, 1937.

1937- Robert Frost. **A Further Range.** NY: Henry Holt, 1936.

1936- Robert P. Tristram Coffin. **Strange Holiness.** New York: Macmillan, 1935.

1935- Audrey Wurdemann. **Bright Ambush.** NY: The John Day Co., 1934.

1934- Robert Hillyer. **Collected Verse.** New York: Alfred A. Knopf, 1933.

1933- Archibald MacLeish. **Conquistador.** Boston: Houghton Mifflin, 1932.

1932- George Dillon. **The Flowering Stone.** NY: Viking, 1931.

1931- Robert Frost. **Collected Poems.** NY: Henry Holt, 1930.

1930- Conrad Aiken**, Selected Poems.** New York, Charles Scribner's Sons, 1929.

1929- Stephen Vincent Benet. **John Browns Body.** Garden City, NY: Doubleday Doran, 1928.

1928- Edwin Arlington Robinson. **Tristram.** New York: Macmillan, 1927.

1927- Leonora Speyer. **Fiddler's Farewell.** New York: Alfred A. Knopf, 1926.

1926- Amy Lowell. **What's O'Clock.** Boston: Houghton Mifflin, 1925.

1925 - Edwin Arlington Robinson. **The Man Who Died Twice.** New York: Macmillan, 1924.

1924- Robert Frost. **New Hampshire: A Poem with Notes and Grace Notes.** NY: Henry Holt, 1923.

1923- Edna St. Vincent Millay. **The Ballad of the Harp-Weaver: A Few Figs from Thistles: Eight Sonnets in American Poetry, 1922. A Miscellany.** NY: Frank Shay, 1922.

1922- Edwin Arlington Robinson. **Collected Poems.** New York: Macmillan, 1921.

1919- Carl Sandburg. **Cornhuskers.** NY: Henry Holt, 1918.

1919- Margaret Widdemer. **Old Road to Paradise.** NY: Henry Holt, 1918.

1918- Sara Teasdale. **Love Songs.** New York: Macmillan, 1918.

National Book Award Winners
Fiction

1950- Nelson Algren. **The Man with the Golden Arm.** Garden City, NY: Doubleday, 1949.

1951- William Faulkner. **Collected Stories.** NY: Random House, 1950.

1952- James Jones. **From Here to Eternity.** NY: Scribner, 1951.

1953- Ralph Ellison. **Invisible Man.** NY: Random House, 1952.

1954- Saul Bellow. **The Adventures of Augie March.** NY: Viking, 1953.

1955- William Faulkner. **A Fable.** NY: Random House, 1954.

1956- John O'Hara. **Ten North Frederick.** NY: Random House, 1955.

1957- Wright Morris. **The Field of Vision.** NY: Harcourt, 1956.

1958- John Cheever. **The Wapshot Chronicle.** NY: Harper, 1957.

1959- Bernard Malamud. **The Magic Barrel. NY**: Farrar, Strauss and Cudahy, 1958.

1960- Philip Roth. **Goodbye, Columbus.** Boston: Houghton Mifflin, 1959.

1961- Conrad Richter. **The Waters of Kronos.** NY: Knopf, 1960.

1962- Walker Percy. **The Moviegoer.** NY: Knopf, 1961.

1963- J.F. Powers **Morte d'Urban.** Garden City, NY: Doubleday, 1962.

1964- John Updike. **The Centaur.** NY: Knopf, 1963.

1965- Saul Bellow. **Herzog.** NY: Viking, 1964.

1966- Katherine Anne Porter. **The Collected Stories of Katherine Anne Porter**. Harcourt, Brace & World, 1965.

1967- Bernard Malamud. **The Fixer**. NY: Farrar, Strauss and Giroux, 1966.

1968- Thornton Wilder **The Eighth Day**. NY: Harper, 1967.

1969- Jerzy Kosinski **Steps**. NY: Random House, 1968.

1970- Joyce Carol Oates. **Them**. New York: Vanguard, 1969.

1971- Saul Bellow. **Mr. Sammler's Planet.** NY: Viking, 1970.

1972- Flannery O'Connor. **The Complete Stories of Flannery O'Connor.** New York: Farrar, Straus and Giroux, 1971.

1973- John Barth. **Chimera.** NY: Random House, 1972.

1973- John Williams. **Augustus**. NY: Viking, 1972.

1974- Thomas Pynchon. **Gravity's Rainbow.** NY: Viking, 1973.

1974- Isaac Bashevis Singer . **A Crown of Feathers**. NY: Farrar, Strauss and Giroux, 1973.

1975- Robert Stone. **Dog Soldiers**. Boston: Houghton-Mifflin, 1974.

1975- Thomas Williams. **The Hair of Harold Roux.** NY: Random House, 1974.

1976- William Gaddis. **J R.** NY: Knopf, 1975.

1977- Wallace Stegner. **The Spectator Bird.** Franklin Center, PA: Franklin Library, 1976.

1978- Mary Lee Settle **Blood Tie.** Boston: Houghton Mifflin, 1977.

1979- Tim O'Brien. **Going After Cacciato.** NY: Delacorte Press/Seymour Press, 1978**.**

1980- William Styron. **Sophie's Choice.** NY: Random House, 1979.

1981- Wright Morris. **Plains Song.** NY: Harper, 1980.

1982- John Updike. **Rabbit is Rich.** NY: Knopf, 1981.

1983- Alice Walker. Walker, Alice. **The Color Purple.** NY: Harcourt, 1982.

1984- Ellen Gilchrist. **Victory Over Japan.** Boston: Little Brown, 1984.

1985- Don DeLillo. **White Noise.** NY: Viking, 1985.

1986- E. L. Doctorow. **World's Fair.** NY: Random House, 1985.

1987- Larry Heinemann. **Paco's Story.** Farrar, Strauss and Giroux, 1986.

1988- Pete Dexter. **Paris Trout.** NY: Random House, 1988.

1989- John Casey. **Spartina.** NY: Knopf, 1989.

1990- Charles Johnson. **Middle Passage.** NY: Atheneum, 1990.

1991- Norman Rush. **Mating.** Westminister, MD: Alfred A. Knopf, 1991.

1992- Cormac McCarthy. **All the Pretty Horses.** NY: Knopf, 1992.

1993- E. Annie Proulx. **The Shipping News.** NY: Scribner, 1993.

1994- William Gaddis **A Frolic of His Own.** NY: Poseidon Press, 1994.

1995- Philip Roth. **Sabbath's Theater.** Boston: Houghton Mifflin, 1995.

1996- Andrea Barrett. **Ship Fever and Other Stories.** New York: Norton, 1996.

1997- Charles Frazier. **Cold Mountain.** NY: Atlantic Monthly Press, 1997.

1998- Alice McDermott. **Charming Billy.** NY: Farrar, Strauss and Giroux, 1998.

1999- Ha Jin. **Waiting.** New York: Pantheon, 1999.

2000- Susan Sontag. **In America.** Franklin Center, PA: Franklin Library, 2000.

2001- Jonathan Franzen. **The Corrections.** NY: Farrar, Strauss and Giroux, 2001.

2002- Julia Glass. **Three Junes.** NY: Pantheon, 2002. '

2003- Shirley Hazzard. **The Great Fire.** Farrar, Strauss and Giroux, 2003.

2004- Lily Tuck. **The News from Paraguay.** NY: HarperCollins, 2004.

2005- William T. Vollmann. **Europe Central.** NY: Viking, 2005.

2006- Richard Powers. **The Echo Maker.** NY: Farrar, Strauss and Giroux, 2006.

2007- Denis Johnson. **Tree of Smoke.** NY: Farrar, Strauss and Giroux, 2007.

2008- Peter Matthiessen. **Shadow Country.** NY: Modern Library Edition. 2008.

The Mann-Booker Prize

2008- Aravind Adiga, **The White Tiger.** London: Atlantic Books, 2008.

2007- Anne Enright. **The Gathering.** London: Jonathan Cape, 2007.

2006- Kiran Desai. **The Inheritance of Loss.** NY: Atlantic Monthly Press, 2006.

2005- John Banville. **The Sea.** London; Picador, 2005.

2004- Alan Hollinghurst. **The Line of Beauty.** London; Picador, 2004.

2003- DBC Pierre. **Vernon God Little.** London: Faber, 2003.

2002- Yann Martel. **Life of Pi.** Toronto: Knopf, 2001.

2001- Peter Carey. **True History of the Kelly Gang.** St Lucia: University of Queensland Press, 2000.

2000- Margaret Atwood. **The Blind Assassin.** Toronto: McClelland & Stewart Inc., 2000.

1999- J.M. Coetzee. **Disgrace.** London: Secker and Warburg, 1999.

1998- Ian McEwan. **Amsterdam.** London: Jonathan Cape, 1998.

1997- Arundhati Roy. **The God of Small Things.** New Delhi, India: IndiaInk, 1997.

1996- Graham Swift. **Last Orders.** London; Picador, 1996.

1995- Pat Barker. **The Ghost Road.** London: Viking, 1995.

1994- James Kelman. **How Late It Was, How Late.** London: Secker & Warburg, 1994.

1993- Roddy Doyle. **Paddy Clarke Ha Ha Ha.** London: Secker and Warburg, 1993.

1992- Michael Ondaatje. **The English Patient.** London: Bloomsbury, 1992.

1992- Barry Unsworth. **Sacred Hunger.** London: Hamish Hamilton, 1992.

1991- Ben Okri. **The Famished Road.** London: Jonathan Cape, 1991.

1990- A.S. Byatt. **Possession: A Romance.** London: Chatto & Windus, 1990.

1989- Kazuo Ishiguro. **The Remains of the Day.** London: Faber, 1989.

1988- Peter Carey. **Oscar and Lucinda.** London: Faber, 1988.

1987- Penelope Lively. **Moon Tiger.** London: Andre Deutsch, 1987.

1986- Kingsley Amis. **The Old Devils.** London: Hutchinson, 1986.

1985- Keri Hulme. **The Bone People.** Wellington, NZ: Spiral, 1983.

1984- Anita Brookner. **Hotel du Lac.** don: Jonathan Cape, 1984.

1983- J.M. Coetzee. **Life & Times of Michael K.** Johannesburg: Ravan Press, 1983.

1982- Thomas Keneally. **Schindler's List.** Sydney: Hodder & Stoughton, 1982.

1981- Salman Rushdie. **Midnight's Children.** London: Jonathan Cape, 1981.

1980- William Golding. **Rites of Passage.** London: Faber, 1980.

1979- Penelope Fitzgerald. **Offshore.** London: Collins, 1979.

1978- Iris Murdoch. **The Sea, The Sea.** London: Chatto & Windus, 1978.

1977- Paul Scott. **Staying On.** London: Heinemann, 1977.

1976- David Storey. **Saville.** London: Jonathan Cape, 1976.

1975- Ruth Prawer Jhabvala. **Heat and Dust.** London: John Murray, 1975.

1974- Nadine Gordimer. **The Conservationist.** London: Jonathan Cape, 1974.

1974- Stanley Middleton. **Holiday.** London: Hutchinson, 1974.
1973- J.G. Farrell. **The Siege of Krishnapur.** London: Weidenfeld & Nicolson,1973.
1972- John Berger. **G.: A Novel.** London: Weidenfeld & Nicolson,1972.
1971- V.S. Naipaul. **In a Free State.** London: Andre Deutsch, 1971.
1970- Bernice Rubens. **The Elected Member.** London: Eyre & Spottiswoode, 1970.
1969- P.H. Newby. **Something to Answer For.** London: Faber, 1968.

The PEN/Faulkner Award for Fiction

2009- Joseph O'Neill. **Netherland.** London: Fourth Estate, 2008
2008- Kate Christensen. **The Great Man.** Garden City, NY: Doubleday, 2007.
2007- Philip Roth. **Everyman.** , Boston/New York: Houghton Mifflin, 2006.
2006- E.L. Doctorow. **The March.** NY: Random House, 2005.
2005- Ha Jin. **War Trash.** NY: Pantheon, 2004.
2004- John Updike. **The Early Stories.** NY: Knopf, 2003.
2003- Sabina Murray. **The Caprices.** Wilmington, MA: Mariner Books, 2002.
2002- Ann Patchett. **Bel Canto.** New York: Harper Collins, 2001.
2001- Phillip Roth. **The Human Stain.** Boston: Houghton Mifflin, 2000.
2000- Ha Jin. **Waiting.** NY: Pantheon, 1999.
1999- Michael Cunningham. **The Hours.** NY: Farrar, Strauss and Giroux, 1998.
1998- Rafi Zabor. **The Bear Comes Home.** New York: Norton, 1997.
1997- Gina Berriault. **Women in Their Beds.** Washington, DC: Counterpoint, 1996.
1996- Richard Ford. **Independence Day.** NY: Knopf, 1995.
1995- David Guterson. **Snow Falling on Cedars.** NY: Harcourt, 1994.
1994- Philip Roth. **Operation Shylock.** NY: Simon & Schuster, 1993.
1993- E. Annie Proulx. **Postcards.** NY: Scribner, 1992.
1992- Don DeLillo. **Mao II.** NY: Viking, 1991.
1991- John Edgar Wideman. **Philadelphia Fire.** NY: Holt, 1990.
1990- E.L. Doctorow. **Billy Bathgate.** Franklin Center, PA: Franklin Library, 1989
1989- James Salter. **Dusk.** San Francisco: North Point Press, 1988.
1988- T. Coraghessan Boyle. **World's End.** NY: Viking, 1987.
1987- Richard Wiley. **Soldiers in Hiding.** Boston: Atlantic Monthly Press, 1986.
1986- Peter Taylor. **The Old Forest.** Garden City, NY: Doubleday/Dial Press, 1985.
1985- Tobias Wolff. **The Barracks Thief.** NY: Ecco, 1984.
1984- John Edgar Wideman. **Sent for You Yesterday.** NY: AVON, 1983.
1983- Toby Olson. **Seaview.** NY: New Directions, 1982.

1982- David Bradley. **The Chaneysville Incident.** NY: Harper & Row, 1981.

1981- Walter Abish. **How German Is It?** NY: New Directions, 1980.

The Randolph Caldecott Medal

2009- Beth Krommes. **The House in the Night.** Wilmington, MA: Houghton Mifflin, 2008.

2008- Brian Selznick. **The Invention of Hugo Cabret.** NY: Scholastic Press, 2007.

2007- David Wiesner, **Flotsam.** New York: Clarion Books. 2007.

2006- Chris Raschka. **The Hello, Goodbye Window.** NY: Michael Di Capua Books Hyperion Books for Children, 2005.

2005- Kevin Henkes. **Kitten's First Full Moon.** NY: Greenwillow Books/HarperCollins, 2004.

2004- Mordicai Gerstein. **The Man Who Walked Between the Towers.** Brookfield, CT: Roaring Brook Press, 2003.

2003- Eric Rohmann. **My Friend Rabbit.** Brookfield, CT: Roaring Brook Press, 2002.

2002- David Wiesner. **The Three Little Pigs.** NY: Clarion Books. 2001.

2001- David Small. **So You Want to be President?** NY: Philomel Books, 2000.

2000- Simms Taback. **Joseph Had a Little Overcoat.** New York: Viking (The Penguin Group), 1999.

1999- Mary Azarian. **Snowflake Bentley**. Boston: Houghton Mifflin Company, 1998.

1998- Paul O. Zelinsky. **Rapunzel.** New York: Dutton Children's Books. 1997.

1997- David Wisniewski. **Golem.** New York: Clarion Books. 1996.

1996- Peggy Rathmann. **Officer Buckle and Gloria**. New York: G. P. Putnam's Sons, 1995.

1995- David Diaz. **Smoky Night**. San Diego, CA & N.Y.: Harcourt Brace, 1994.

1994- Allen Say. **Grandfather's Journey.** Boston: Houghton Mifflin Company, 1993.

1993- Emily Arnold McCully. **Mirette on the High Wire.** New York: G. P. Putnam's Sons, 1992.

1992- David Wiesner. **Tuesday.** NY: Clarion Books. 1991.

1991- David Macaulay **Black and White.** Boston: Houghton Mifflin Company, 1990.

1990- Ed Young. **Lon Po Po: A Red Riding Hood Story from China.** NY: Philomel Books, 1989.

1989- Stephen Gammell. **Song and Dance Man.** NY: Knopf, 1988.

1988- John Schoenherr. **Owl Moon.** John Schoenherr NY: Philomel Books, 1987.

1987- Richard Egielski. **Hey, Al!** NY: Farrar, Strauss and Giroux, 1986.

1986- Chris Van Allsburg. **The Polar Express.** Boston: Houghton Mifflin Company, 1985.

1985- Trina S. Hyman. **St. George and the Dragon.** Boston: Little Brown, 1984.

1984- Alice & Martin Provensen. **The Glorious Flight.** New York: The Viking Press, 1983.

1983- Marcia Brown. **Shadow.** NY: Scribner's., 1982.

1982- Chris Van Allsburg. **Jumanji.** Boston: Houghton Mifflin Company, 1981.

1981- Arnold Lobel. **Fables.** New York: Harper & Row, 1980.

1980- Barbara Cooney. **Ox-Cart Man.** New York: The Viking Press, 1979.

1979- Paul Goble. **The Girl Who Loved Wild Horses.** Scarsdale, NY: Bradbury Press, 1978.

1978- Peter Spier. **Noah's Ark.** Garden City, NY: Doubleday, 1977.

1977- Leo Dillon. **Ashanti to Zulu: African Traditions.** NY: The Dial Press, 1976.

1976- Leo Dillon. **Why Mosquitoes Buzz in People's Ears.** NY: The Dial Press, 1975.

1975- Gerald McDermott. **Arrow to the Sun: A Pueblo Indian Tale.** New York: The Viking Press, 1974.

1974- Margot Zemach. **Duffy and the Devil.** NY: Farrar, Strauss and Giroux, 1973.

1973- Blair Lent. **The Funny Little Woman.** NY: Dutton, 1972.

1972- Nonny Hogrogian. **One Fine Day.** NY: Macmillan, 1971.

1971- Gail E. Haley. **A Story--A Story.** NY: Macmillan, 1970.

1970- William Steig. **Sylvester and the Magic Pebble.** NY: Windmill/E.P. Dutton, 1969.

1969- Uri Shulevitz. **The Fool of the World and the Flying Ship.** NY: Farrar, Strauss and Giroux, 1968.

1968- Ed Emberley. **Drummer Hoff.** E NY: Simon & Schuster, 1967.

1967- Evaline Ness. **Sam, Bangs & Moonshine.** NY: Henry Holt, 1966.

1966- Nonny Hogrogian. **Always Room for One More.** NY: Henry Holt, 1966.

1965- Beni Montresor. **May I Bring a Friend?** New York: Atheneum, 1964.

1964- Maurice Sendak. **Where the Wild Things Are.** NY: Harper Row, 1963.

1963- Ezra J. Keats. **The Snowy Day.** New York: The Viking Press, 1962.

1962- Marcia Brown. **Once a Mouse. . .** NY: Scribner, 1961.

1961- Nicholas Sidjakov. **Boushka and the Three Kings.** Berkeley, CA: Parnassus Press. 1960.

1960- Maria H. Ets. **Nine Days to Christmas.** New York: The Viking Press, 1959.

1959- Barbara Cooney. **Chanticleer and the Fox.** New York: Thomas Y. Crowell Company, 1958.

1958- Robert McCloskey. **Time of Wonder.** New York: The Viking Press, 1957.

1957- Marc Simont. **A Tree Is Nice.** New York: Harper & Row, 1956.
1956- Feodor Rojankovsky. **Frog Went A-Courtin'.** NY: Harcourt, 1955.
1955- Marcia Brown. **Cinderella.** NY: Macmillan, 1954.
1954- Ludwig Bemelmans. **Madeline's Rescue.** New York: The Viking Press, 1953.
1953- Lynd Ward. **The Biggest Bear.** Boston: Houghton Mifflin Company, 1952.
1952- Nicolas Mordvinoff. **Finders Keepers.** NY: Harcourt, 1951.
1951- Katherine Milhous. **The Egg Tree**. NY: Macmillan, 1950.
1950- Leo Politi. **Song of the Swallows.** NY: Scribner, 1949.
1949- Berta Hader. **The Big Snow.** NY: Macmillan, 1948.
1948- Roger Duvoisin. **White Snow, Bright Snow.** NY: Lee & Shepard Books, 1947.
1947- Leonard Weisgard. *The Little Island.* Garden City, NY: Doubleday, 1946.
1946- Maud Petersham. **The Rooster Crows**. NY: Macmillan, 1945.
1945- Elizabeth O. Jones. **Prayer for a Child.** Eli NY: Macmillan, 1944.
1944- Louis Slobodkin. **Many Moons**. NY: Harcourt, 1943.
1943- Virginia L. Burton. **The Little House** Boston: Houghton Mifflin Company, 1942.
1942- Robert McCloskey. **Make Way for Ducklings**. New York: The Viking Press, 1941.
1941- Robert Lawson **They Were Strong and Good.** New York: The Viking Press, 1940.
1940- Ingri d'Aulaire. **Abraham Lincoln.** Garden City, NY: Doubleday, 1939.
1939- Thomas Handforth. **Mei Li.** Garden City, NY: Doubleday, 1938.
1938- Dorothy Lathrop. **Animals of the Bible.** NY: Frederick A. Stokes, 1937.

The John Newbery Medal

2009- Neil Gaiman. **The Graveyard Book.** NY: HarperCollins, 2008.
2008- Laura Amy Schlitz. **Good Masters! Sweet Ladies! Voices from a Medieval Village.** NY: Candlewick Press., 2007.
2007- Susan Patron. **The Higher Power of Lucky.** N.Y.: Atheneum 2006.
2006- Lynne Rae Perkins. **Criss Cross.** NY: Greenwillow Books, 2005.
2005- Cynthia Kadohata. **Kira-Kira.** Cynthia Kadohata (N.Y.: Atheneum 2004.
2004- Kate DiCamillo. **The Tale of Despereaux.** Cambridge, MA: Candlewick Press. 2003.
2003- Avi. **Crispin: The Cross of Lead**. NY.: Hyperion Books for Children, 2002.
2002- Linda Sue Park. **A Single Shard.** NY: Clarion Books, 2001.

2001- Richard Peck. **A Year Down Yonder.** NY: The Dial Press, 2000.

2000- Christopher Paul Curtis. **Bud, Not Buddy.** NY: Delacorte 1999.

1999- Louis Sachar. **Holes.** NY: Farrar, Strauss and Giroux, 1998.

1998- Karen Hesse. **Out of the Dust.** New York: Scholastic Press, 1997.

1997- E.L. Konigsburg. **The View from Saturday.** N.Y.: Atheneum, 1997.

1996- Karen Cushman. **The Midwife's Apprentice.** NY: Clarion Books, 1995.

1995- Sharon Creech. **Walk Two Moons.** NY: HarperCollins, 1994.

1994- Lois Lowry. **The Giver.** Boston: Houghton Mifflin Company, 1993.

1993- Cynthia Rylant. **Missing May.** NY: Orchard Books, 1992.

1992- Phyllis Reynolds Naylor. **Shiloh.** N.Y.: Atheneum, 1991.

1991- , Jerry Spinelli. **Maniac Magee.** Boston: Little Brown, 1990.

1990- Lois Lowry. **Number the Stars.** Boston: Houghton Mifflin Company, 1989.

1989- Paul Fleischman. **Joyful Noise: Poems for Two Voices.** NY: Harper & Row, 1988.

1988- Russell Freedman. **Lincoln: A Photobiography.** Boston: Houghton Mifflin Company, 1987.

1987- Sid Fleischman. **The Whipping Boy.** New York: Greenwillow Books, 1986.

1986- Patricia MacLachlan. **Sarah, Plain and Tall.** NY: Harper & Row, 1985.

1985- Robin McKinley. **The Hero and the Crown.** New York: Greenwillow Books, 1984.

1984- Beverly Cleary. **Dear Mr. Henshaw.** NY: William Morrow, 1983.

1983- Cynthia Voigt. **Dicey's Song.** N.Y.: Atheneum, 1982.

1982- Nancy Willard. **A Visit to William Blake's Inn: Poems for Innocent and Experienced Travelers.** NY: Harcourt, 1980.

1981- Katherine Paterson. **Jacob Have I Loved.** New York: Thomas Y. Crowell, 1980.

1980- Joan W. Blos. **A Gathering of Days: A New England Girl's Journal, 1830-32.** NY: Scribner, 1979.

1979- Ellen Raskin. **The Westing Game.** New York. E.P. Dutton, 1978.

1978- Katherine Paterson. **Bridge to Terabithia.** New York: Thomas Y. Crowell Company, 1977.

1977- Mildred Taylor. **Roll of Thunder, Hear My Cry.** NY: The Dial Press, 1976.

1976- Susan Cooper. **The Grey King.** N.Y.: Atheneum, 1975.

1975- Virginia Hamilton. **M.C. Higgins the Great.** NY: Macmillan, 1974.

1974- Paula Fox. **The Slave Dancer.** New York: Bradbury Press, 1973.

1973- Jean C. George. **Julie of the Wolves.** NY: Harper & Row, 1972.

1972- Robert C. O'Brien. **Mrs. Frisby and the Rats of NIMH**. N.Y.: Atheneum, 1971.

1971- Betsy C. Byars. **Summer of the Swans.** New York: The Viking Press, 1970.

1970- William Armstrong. **Sounder**. William Armstrong NY: Harper & Row, 1969.

1969- Lloyd Alexander. **The High King**. NY: Henry Holt, 1968.

1968- E.L. Konigsburg. **From the Mixed-Up Files of Mrs. Basil E. Frankweiler**. N.Y.: Atheneum, 1967.

1967- Irene Hunt. **Up a Road Slowly**. Chicago: Follett, 1966.

1966- Elizabeth B. de Trevino. **I, Juan de Pareja,** NY: Farrar, Strauss and Giroux, 1965.

1965- Maia Wojciechowska. **Shadow of a Bull.** N.Y.: Atheneum, 1964.

1964- Emily C. Neville. **It's Like This, Cat.** NY: Harper & Row, 1963.

1963- Madeleine L'Engle. **A Wrinkle in Time**. NY: Farrar, Strauss and Giroux, 1962.

1962- Elizabeth G. Speare. **The Bronze Bow**. Boston: Houghton Mifflin Company, 1961.

1961- Scott O'Dell. **Island of the Blue Dolphins.** Boston: Houghton Mifflin Company, 1960.

1960- Joseph Krumgold. **Onion John.** New York: Thomas Y. Crowell Company, 1959.

1959 - Elizabeth G. Speare. **The Witch of Blackbird Pond**. Boston: Houghton Mifflin Company, 1958.

1958- Harold Keith. **Rifles for Watie**. NY: Harper & Row, 1957.

1957- Virginia Sorensen. **Miracles on Maple Hill.** NY: Harcourt, 1956.

1956- Jean L. Latham. **Carry On, Mr. Bowditch.** Boston: Houghton Mifflin Company, 1955.

1955- Meindert De Jong. **The Wheel on the School.** NY: Harper & Row, 1954.

1954- Joseph Krumgold. **And Now Miguel.** J New York: Thomas Y. Crowell Company, 1953.

1953- Ann N. Clark. **Secret of the Andes**. New York: The Viking Press, 1952.

1952- Eleanor Estes. **Ginger Pye**. NY: Harcourt, 1951.

1951- Elizabeth Yates. **Amos Fortune, Free Man**. New York. E.P. Dutton, 1950.

1950- Marguerite de Angeli. **The Door in the Wall: Story of Medieval London.** Garden City, NY: Doubleday, 1949.

1949- Marguerite Henry. **King of the Wind.** Chicago: Rand McNally, 1948.

1948- William Pene du Bois. **The Twenty-One Balloons**. New York: The Viking Press, 1947.

1947- Carolyn S. Bailey. **Miss Hickory**. New York: The Viking Press, 1946.

1946- Lois Lenski. **Strawberry Girl**. Philadelphia: J. B. Lippincott, 1945.

1945- Robert Lawson. **Rabbit Hill.** New York: The Viking Press, 1944.

1944- Ester Forbes. **Johnny Tremain**. Boston: Houghton Mifflin Company, 1943.

1943- Elizabeth J. Gray. **Adam of the Road.** New York: The Viking Press, 1942.

1942- Walter D. Edmonds. **The Matchlock Gun.** New York : Dodd, Mead, 1941.

1941- Armstrong Sperry. **Call It Courage.** New York: Macmillan, 1940.

1940- James Daugherty. **Daniel Boone.** New York: The Viking Press, 1939.

1939- Elizabeth Enright. **Thimble Summer.** NY: Henry Holt, 1938.

1938- Kate Seredy. **The White Stag.** New York: The Viking Press, 1937.

1937- Ruth Sawyer. **Roller Skates.** New York: The Viking Press, 1936.

1936- Carol R. Brink. **Caddie Woodlawn.** New York: Macmillan, 1935.

1935- Monica Shannon. **Dobry.** New York: The Viking Press, 1934.

1934- Cornelia Meigs. **Invincible Louisa**. Boston: Little Brown, 1933.

1933- Elizabeth F. Lewis. **Young Fu of the Upper Yangtze.** NY: Henry Holt, 1932.

1932- Laura A. Armer. **Waterless Mountain.** NY: Longmans Green 1931.

1931- Elizabeth Coatsworth. **The Cat Who Went to Heaven**. New York: Macmillan, 1930.

1930- Rachel Field. **Hitty, Her First Hundred Years**. New York: Macmillan, 1929.

1929- Eric P. Kelly. **The Trumpeter of Krakow.** New York: Macmillan, 1928.

1928 - Dhan G. Mukerji. **Gay-Neck: The Story of a Pigeon.** New York. E.P. Dutton, 1927.

1927- Will James. **Smoky, the Cow Horse.** New York, Charles Scribner's Sons, 1926.

1926- Arthur B. Chrisman. **Shen of the Sea**. New York. E.P. Dutton, 1925.

1925- Charles J. Finger. **Tales from Silver Lands.** Garden City, NY: Doubleday, 1924.

1924- Charles B. Hawes. **The Dark Frigate**. Boston: Little Brown, 1923.

1923- Hugh Lofting. **The Voyages of Doctor Dolittle.** NY: Frederick A. Stokes, 1922.

1922- Hendrik W. Van Loon. **The Story of Mankind.** NY: Boni & Liveright, 1921.

Edgar Best Novel Award

2008- John Hart. **Soul Patch.** NY: St. Martin's, 2007.

2007- Jason Goodwin. **The Janissary Tree.** NY: Farrar, Strauss and Giroux, 2006.

2006- Jess Walter. **Citizen Vince.** NY: Regan Books, 2005.

2005- T. Jefferson Parker. **California Girl.** Scranton, PA: William Morrow, 2004.

2004- Ian Rankin. **Resurrection Men.** London. Orion: 2001.

2003- S. J. Rozan. **Winter and Night.** NY: St. Martin's, 2002.

2002- T. Jefferson Parker. **Silent Joe.** Boston: Hyperion, 2001.

2001- Joe R. Lansdale. **The Bottoms.** NY: Mysterious Press, 2000.

2000- Jan Burke. **Bones.** Riverside, NJ: Simon & Schuster, 1999.

1999- Robert Clark. **Mr. White's Confession.** New York: Picador, 1998.

1998- James Lee Burke. **Cimarron Rose.** London. Orion: 1997.

1997- Thomas Cook. **The Chatham School Affair.** New York: Bantam, 1996.

1996- Dick Francis. **Come to Grief.** London: Michael Joseph, 1995.

1995- Mary Walker. **The Red Scream.** Garden City, NY: Doubleday, 1994.

1994- Minette Walters. **The Sculptress.** London: Macmillan 1993.

1993- Margaret Maron. **Bootlegger's Daughter.** NY: Mysterious Press, 1992.

1992 - Lawrence Block. **A Dance at the Slaughterhouse.** Scranton, PA: William Morrow, 1991.

1991- Julie Smith. **New Orleans Mourning.** NY: St. Martin's, 1990.

1990- James Lee Burke. **Black Cherry Blues.** Boston: Little Brown, 1989.

1989- Stuart Kaminsky. **A Cold Red Sunrise.** New York, Charles Scribner's Sons, 1988.

1988- Aaron Elkins. **Old Bones.** NY: Mysterious Press, 1987.

1987- Barbara Vine. **A Dark Adapted Eye.** London: Viking, 1986.

1986- L. R. Wright. **The Suspect.** NY: Viking, 1985.

1985- Ross Thomas. **Briarpatch.** NY: Simon & Schuster, 1984.

1984- Elmore Leonard. **La Brava.** NY: Arbor House, 1983.

1983- Rick Boyer. **Billingsgate Shoal.** Boston: Houghton Mifflin Company, 1982.

1982- William Bayer. **Peregrine.** NY: Congdon & Lattes, 1981.

1981- Dick Francis. **Whip Hand.** London: Michael Joseph, 1979.

1980- Arthur Maling. **The Rheingold Route.** New York: Harper & Row, 1979.

1979- Ken Follet. **The Eye of the Needle.** NY: Arbor House, 1978.

1978- William H. Hallahan. **Catch Me Kill Me.** Indianapolis, IN: Bobbs-Merrill, 1977.

1977- Robert B. Parker. **Promised Land.** Boston: Houghton Mifflin Company, 1976.

1976- Brian Garfield. **Hopscotch.** , New York: M. Evans, 1975.

1975- Jon Cleary. **Peter's Pence.** London: Collins, 1974.

1974- Tony Hillerman. **Dance Hall of the Dead.** New York: Harper & Row, 1973.

1973- Warren Kiefer. **The Lingala Code.** NY: Random House, 1972.

1972- Frederick Forsyth. **The Day of the Jackal.** NY: Viking, 1971.

1971- Maj Sjöwall and Per Wahlöö. **The Laughing Policeman.** New York: Pantheon Books, 1970.

1970- Dick Francis. **Forfeit.** London: Michael Joseph, 1968.

1969 - Jeffrey Hudson. **A Case of Need.** New York: NAL/World, 1968.

1968- Donald E. Westlake. **God Save the Mark.** NY: Random House, 1967.

1967- Nicolas Freeling. **The King of the Rainy Country.** London: Gollancz, 1966.

1966- Adam Hall. **The Quiller Memorandum.** London: Collins, 1965.

1965- John Le Carré. **The Spy Who Came in from the Cold.** London: Gollancz, 1963.

1964- Eric Ambler. **The Light of Day.** London: William Heinemann, 1962.

1963- Ellis Peters. **Death and the Joyful Woman.** London: Collins/Crime Club, 1961.

1962- J. J. Marric. **Gideon's Fire.** London: Hodder & Stoughton, 1961.

1961- Julian Symons. **The Progress of a Crime.** London: Collins/Crime Club, 1960.

1960- Celia Fremlin. **The Hours Before Dawn.** London: Gollancz, 1958.

1959- Stanley Ellin. **The Eighth Circle.** NY: Random House, 1958.

1958- Ed Lacy. **Room to Swing.** New York: Harper, 1957.

1957- Charlotte Armstrong. **A Dram of Poison.** London: Peter Davies, 1956.

1956- Margaret Millar. **Beast in View.** NY: Random House, 1955.

1955- Raymond Chandler. **The Long Goodbye.** Boston: Houghton Mifflin, 1954.

1954- Charlotte Jay. **Beat Not the Bones.** New York: Harper, 1953.

Hugo Best Novel Award

2009- Neil Gaiman. **The Graveyard Book.** NY: HarperCollins, 2008.

2008- Michael Chabon. **The Yiddish Policemen's Union.** NY: HarperCollins, 2007.

2007- Vernor Vinge. **Rainbows End.** New York: Tor, 2006.

2006- Robert Charles Wilson. **Spin.** New York: Tor, 2005.

2005- Susanna Clarke. **Jonathan Strange & Mr. Norrell.** London, Bloomsbury Publishing , 2004.

2004- Lois McMaster Bujold. **Paladin of Souls.** NY: HarperCollins/EOS, 2003.

2003- Robert J. Sawyer. **Hominids.** New York: Tor, 2002.
2002- Neil Gaiman. **American Gods.** Dresden, TN: Avon Books, 2001.
2001- J.K. Rowling. **Harry Potter and the Goblet of Fire.** London, Bloomsbury Publishing , 2000.
2000- Vernor Vinge. **A Deepness in the Sky.** New York: Tor/Tom Doherty Associates, 1999.
1999- Connie Willis. **To Say Nothing of the Dog.** New York: Bantam Books, 1997.
1998- Joe Haldeman. **Forever Peace.** New York: Ace Books, 1997.
1997- Kim Stanley Robinson. **Blue Mars.** London: HarperCollins/Voyager, 1996.
1996- Neal Stephenson. **Diamond Age.** New York: Bantam Books, 1995.
1995- Lois McMaster Bujold. **Mirror Dance.** Riverdale, NY: Baen Publishing Enterprises, 1994.
1994- Kim Stanley Robinson. **Green Mars.** London: HarperCollins, 1993.
1993- Vernor Vinge. **Fire Upon the Deep.** New York: Tor, 1992.
1993- Connie Willis. **Doomsday Book.** New York: Bantam Books, 1992.
1992- Lois McMaster Bujold. **Barrayar.** Riverdale, NY: Baen Publishing Enterprises, 1991.
1991- Lois McMaster Bujold. **Vor Game.** Riverdale, NY: Baen Publishing Enterprises, 1990.
1990- Dan Simmons. **Hyperion.** Garden City, NY: Doubleday, 1989.
1989- C. J. Cherryh. **Cyteen.** New York: Warner Books, 1988.
1988- David Brin. **Uplift War.** West Bloomfield, MI: Phantasia Press, 1987.
1987- Orson Scott Card. **Speaker for the Dead.** New York: Tor/Tom Doherty Associates, 1986.
1986- Orson Scott Card. **Ender's Game.** New York: Tor, 1985.
1985- William Gibson. **Neuromancer.** London: Gollancz, 1984.
1984- David Brin. **Startide Rising.** New York: Bantam Books, 1983.
1983- Isaac Asimov. **Foundation's Edge.** Garden City, NY: Doubleday, 1982.
1982- C. J. Cherryh. **Downbelow Station.** NY: DAW, 1981.
1981- Joan D. Vinge. **Snow Queen.** New York: The Dial Press, 1980.
1980- Arthur C. Clarke. **Fountains of Paradise.** London: Gollancz, 1979.
1979- Vonda McIntyre. **Dreamsnake.** Boston: Houghton Mifflin Company, 1978.
1978- Frederik Pohl. **Gateway.** New York: St. Martin's Press, 1977.
1977- Kate Wilhelm. **Where Late the Sweet Birds Sang.** New York: Harper & Row, 1976.
1976- Joe Haldeman. **Forever War.** New York: St. Martin's Press, 1974.
1975- Ursula K. LeGuin. **Dispossessed.** New York: Harper & Row, 1974.

1974- Arthur C. Clarke. **Rendezvous with Rama.** London: Gollancz, 1973.

1973- Isaac Asimov. **Gods Themselves.** Garden City, NY: Doubleday, 1972.

1972- Philip Jose Farmer. **To Your Scattered Bodies Go.** New York: G. P. Putnam's Sons, 1971.

1971- Larry Niven. **Ringworld.** NY: Ballantine Books, 1970.

1970- Ursula K. LeGuin. **Left Hand of Darkness.** NY: Walker and Co, 1969.

1969- John Brunner. **Stand on Zanzibar.** Garden City, NY: Doubleday, 1968.

1968- Roger Zelazny. **Lord of Light.** Garden City, NY: Doubleday, 1967.

1967- Robert A. Heinlein. **Moon is a Harsh Mistress.** New York: G. P. Putnam's Sons, 1966.

1966- Roger Zelazny. **... and Call Me Conrad.** NY: ACE, 1965.

1966- Frank Herbert. **Dune.** Philadelphia, Chilton, 1965.

1965- Fritz Leiber. **Wanderer.** NY: Walker and Co, 1964.

1964- Clifford D. Simak. **Way Station.** Garden City, NY: Doubleday, 1963.

1963- Philip K. Dick. **Man in the High Castle.** New York: G. P. Putnam's Sons, 1962.

1962- Robert A. Heinlein. **Stranger in a Strange Land.** New York: G. P. Putnam's Sons, 1961.

1961- Walter M. Miller, Jr. **A Canticle for Leibowitz.** Philadelphia & NY: J. B. Lippincott Company, 1960.

1960- Robert A. Heinlein. **Starship Troopers.** New York: G. P. Putnam's Sons, 1959.

1959- James Blish. **Case of Conscience.** NY: Ballantine, 1958.

1958- Fritz Leiber. **The Big Time.** London: Severn House, 1961 (*Galaxy* Mar., Apr. 1958)

1956- Robert A. Heinlein. **Double Star.** Garden City, NY: Doubleday, 1956.

1955- Mark Clifton. **They'd Rather Be Right.** New York: Gnome Press, 1957.
(*Astounding*, 1954)

1953- Alfred Bester. **The Demolished Man.** Chicago: Shasta Publishers, 1953.

Retro HUGO Awards

1946- Isaac Asimov. **The Mule.** *Astounding* Nov., Dec. 1945. Included in: **Foundation and Empire.** NY: Gnome Press, 1952.

1951- Robert A. Heinlein. **Farmer in the Sky.** New York: G. P. Putnam's Sons, 1950.

1954- Ray Bradbury. **Fahrenheit 451.** New York: Ballantine Books, 1953.

Nebula Award Winning Novels

2008- Ursula K. Le Guin. **Powers.** NY: Harcourt, 2007.

2007- Michael Chabon. **The Yiddish Policemen's Union.** NY: HarperCollins, 2007.

2006- Jack McDevitt. **Seeker.** NY: Ace, 2005.

2005- Joe Haldeman. **Camouflage.** NY: Ace, 2004.

2004- Lois McMaster Bujold. **Paladin of Souls.** NY: HarperCollins/EOS, 2003.

2003- Elizabeth Moon. **The Speed of Dark.** NY: Ballantine, 2002.

2002- Neil Gaiman. **American Gods.** Dresden, TN: Avon Books, 2001.

2001- Catherine Asaro. **The Quantum Rose.** New York: Tor, 2000.

2000- Greg Bear. **Darwin's Radio.** New York.: Del Rey/Ballantine., 1999.

1999- Octavia E. Butler. **Parable of the Talents.** New York / Toronto: Seven Stories Press, 1998.

1998- Joe Haldeman. **Forever Peace.** NY: Ace, 1997.

1997- Vonda N. McIntyre. **The Moon and the Sun.** NY: Pocket Books 1997.

1996- Nicola Griffith. **Slow River.** New York.: Del Rey/Ballantine., 1995.

1995- Robert J. Sawyer. **The Terminal Experiment.** NY: HarperCollins, 1995.

1994- Greg Bear. **Moving Mars.** New York: Tor, 1993.

1993- Kim Stanley Robinson. **Red Mars.** London: HarperCollins, 1992.

1992- Connie Willis. **Doomsday Book.** New York: Bantam Books, 1992.

1991- Michael Swanwick. **Stations of the Tide.** New York: William Morrow, 1991.

1990- Ursula K. Le Guin. **Tehanu: The Last Book of Earthsea.** New York, Atheneum, 1990.

1989- Elizabeth Ann Scarborough. **The Healer's War.** Garden City, NY: Doubleday, 1988.

1988- Lois McMaster Bujold. **Falling Free.** Riverdale, NY: Baen Publishing Enterprises, 1988.

1987- Pat Murphy. **The Falling Woman.** New York: Tor/Tom Doherty Associates, 1986.

1986- Orson Scott Card. **Speaker for the Dead.** New York: Tor/Tom Doherty Associates, 1986.

1985- Orson Scott Card. **Ender's Game.** New York: Tor, 1985.

1984- William Gibson. **Neuromancer.** London: Gollancz, 1984.

1983- David Brin. **Startide Rising.** New York: Bantam Books, 1983.

1982- Michael Bishop. **No Enemy But Time.** New York: Timescape / Simon and Schuster, 1982.

1981- Gene Wolfe. **The Claw of the Conciliator.** New York: Timescape / Simon and Schuster, 1981.

1980- Gregory Benford. **Timescape.** New York: Simon and Schuster, 1980.

1979- Arthur C. Clarke. **Fountains of Paradise.** London: Gollancz, 1979.

1978- Vonda McIntyre. **Dreamsnake.** Boston: Houghton Mifflin Company, 1978.

1977- Frederik Pohl. **Gateway.** New York: St. Martin's Press, 1977.

1976- Frederik Pohl. **Man Plus.** NY: Random House, 1976.

1975- Joe Haldeman. **Forever War.** New York: St. Martin's Press, 1974.

1974- Ursula K. LeGuin. **Dispossessed.** New York: Harper & Row, 1974.

1973- Arthur C. Clarke. **Rendezvous with Rama.** London: Gollancz, 1973.

1972- Isaac Asimov. **Gods Themselves.** Garden City, NY: Doubleday, 1972.

1971- Robert Silverberg. **A Time of Changes.** Garden City, NY: Doubleday, 1971.

1970- Larry Niven. **Ringworld.** NY: Ballantine Books, 1970.

1969- Ursula K. LeGuin. **Left Hand of Darkness.** NY: Walker and Co, 1969.

1968- Alexei Panshin. **Rite of Passage.** London: Sidgwick & Jackson, 1968.

1967- Samuel R. Delany. **The Einstein Intersection.** NY: ACE, 1967.

1966- Samuel R. Delany. **Babel-17.** NY: ACE, 1966.

1966- Daniel Keyes. **Flowers for Algernon.** NY: Harcourt, 1966.

1965- Frank Herbert. **Dune.** Philadelphia, Chilton, 1965.

Identify the Book

Now here's the real insanity. The book fits the first edition chart, you've identified the pseudonym of the author, and it's a prize-winner. All good, right? Well, not exactly.

You see publishers, and the people that work for them, are the world's biggest screw-ups, and they keep trying to cover that up. They missed a quote on the dust jacket, so they print a wrap around band. "Man" on page twenty-seven somehow got printed "Maam" and they changed it after they printed a thousand books or so. They can't seem to get it right, so as collectors, people have to search out these screw-ups in bibliographies and other references like this one. I have a passle below, enough to get you started, but remember, book collectors are stuck with publishers, and all the original blond jokes were initially about publishers, until people realized that blondes are smarter than publishers.

Ackerley, J.R. **My Father and Myself.** New York: Coward-McCann, 1969. First Issue has a wrap around band with a Capote quote.

Agee, James. **A Death in the Family**. NY: McDowell Obolensky, 1957. "Walking" for "Waking" on page 80.

Akers, Floyd (L. Frank Baum). **The Boy Fortune Hunters in Panama.** Chicago: Reilly and Britton, 1908. Open book device above imprint on the title page is first issue.
_____ (L. Frank Baum). **The Boy Fortune Hunters in the South Seas.** Chicago: Reilly and Britton, 1911. Ads list "The Darling Twins", "Annabel", and the first six Aunt Jane's Neices titles.

Aldrich, Thomas Bailey. **Story Of A Bad Boy.** Boston: Fields, Osgood, & Co 1870. First state with p. 14, line 20, reading "scattered" for " scatters, " and p. 197, line 10, "abroad" for "aboard.

Alexander, E. P. **Military Memoirs of a Confederate.**
New York: Charles Scribners, 1907. Black cloth lettered in gilt in first issue.

Alger, Horatio, Jr. **Ragged Dick; Or, Street Life in New York With the Boot-Blacks**. Boston: Loring, 1868. First state with "Fame and Fortune" announced for December and Dick alone on the decorative title page.

Algren, Nelson. **The Man with the Golden Arm.** Garden City, NY: Doubleday, 1949. First Edition stated, light gray cloth with red and green lettering on the spine and green top stain, endpapers are green. 1st issue dust jacket has three reviews - Chicago Sun, Malcolm Cowley, and Chicago Tribune

Allen, Hervey. **Anthony Adverse.** New York.: Farrar and Rinehart. 1933. Page 352, line 6 "Zavier", page 397, line 22 "found found", page 1086, line 18 "ship".

Anderson, Sherwood. **Winesburg, Ohio. A Group of Tales of Ohio Small Town Life.** New York: B.W. Heubsch, 1919. First edition, first issue, with line 5 of p.86 reading "lay" and with broken type in "the" in line 3 of p.251. Top edge stained yellow; map on front pastedown.

Anonymous (L. Frank Baum). **The Last Egyptian.** Philadelphia:Edward Stern, 1908. The verso carries no imprint and states "Published May 1, 1908".

Ansay, A. Manette. **Vinegar Hill.** NY: Viking, 1994. States "First published in 1994 by Viking Penguin" with number line "1 3 5 7 9 10 8 6 4 2".

Anson, Jay. **The Amityville Horror.** Englewood Cliffs, NJ: Prentice Hall, 1977. Number line "10 9 8 7 6 5 4 3 2 1" in brown cloth. 1st Issue dust jacket has four blurbs.

Arthurs, Stanley. **The American Historical Scene.** Philadelphia: University of Pennsylvania Press, 1935. Limited Edition: 100 Copies. Contains an original water color by Stanley Arthurs.

Atwood, Margaret. **The Blind Assassin.** Toronto: McClelland and Stewart, 1996. Number line "1 2 3 4 5   04 03 02 01 00".

Auel, Jean. **The Clan of the Cave Bear.** NY: Crown, 1980. First Edition stated with "10 9 8 7 6 5 4 3 2 1" number line.

Bachman, Richard. **The Long Walk.** NY: Signet, 1979. PBO "First Signet Printing, July, 1979" stated with number line 1 2 3 4 5 6 7 8 9.
_____. **Rage.** NY: Signet, 1977. PBO "First Signet Printing, September, 1977" stated with number line 1 2 3 4 5 6 7 8 9. Signet #W7645.

Baker, Kevin. **Dreamland.** NY: HarperCollins, 1999. FIRST EDITION stated with number line 10 9 8 7 6 5 4 3 2 1.
_____. **Paradise Alley.** NY: HarperCollins, 2002. FIRST EDITION stated with number line 10 9 8 7 6 5 4 3 2 1.
_____. **Sometimes You See It Coming.** NY: Crown, 1993. First Edition stated with number line "10 9 8 7 6 5 4 3 2 1" in light blue boards with blue metallic lettering and an orange cloth spine. 1st issue dust jacket lacks reviews.

Baldwin, James. **Go Tell it on the Mountain.** NY: Knopf, 1953. FIRST EDITION stated.

Barnes, Djuna. **Ryder.** New York: Horace Liveright, 1928. The first printing states "limited to 3000 Copies."

Barnes, Margaret Ayer. **Years of Grace.** Boston: Houghton Mifflin, 1930. The title page date must match the copyright date (1930).

Barney, James. **Tales of Apache Warfare.** Phoenix, AZ: James Barney, 1933. In printed wraps.

Barrett, Andrea. **Ship Fever and Other Stories**. New York: Norton, 1996. FIRST EDITION stated with number line "1 2 3 4 5 6 7 8 9 0".

Barrie, James M. **When a Man's Single. A Tale of Literary Life.** London: Hodder & Stoughton 1888. The first issue has two pages of ads after the text.
_____. **A Tillyloss Scandal.** New York: Lovell Coryell, 1893. This is an American Pirate, cobbled together from magazine pieces. The first edition carries the address: "43, 45 and 47 East Tenth Street" and was issued in buff colored wraps.
_____. **Auld Licht Idyls.** London: Hodder & Stoughton 1888. The first issue has two pages of ads after the text.
_____. **The Little Minister. (**Three Volumes) London: Cassell & Co., 1891. The text runs to the last page in all three volumes and the end of Volume One carries 16 pages of ads.
_____. **Sentimental Tommy**. London: Cassell & Co., 1896. The date code on the advertising is "6G-8.96".

Barth, John. **Chimera.** NY: Random House, 1972. Signed edition limited to 300 copies in red cloth boards and silver lettering issued with a gray paper slipcase. The first trade edition has "First Edition" with a number line of "9 8 7 6 5 4 3 2 ". 1st dust jacket has no blurbs.
_____. **Giles Goat-Boy or, The Revised New Syllabus.** Garden City, NY: Doubleday & Co., 1966. Limited Edition of 250 Copies, First trade edition:: First state has "H18" at the bottom of the last page and lacks a "First Edition" notice on the verso.

Baum, L. Frank. **Mother Goose in Prose.** Chicago: Way and Williams, 1897. Bound in 16 page signatures except the last two which are 8 and 4.
_____. **The Marvelous Land of Oz**. Chicago: Reilly and Britton, 1904. The cover title is printed in blue in first issue.
_____. **Ozma of Oz.** Chicago: Reilly and Britton, 1907. First state is believed to be missing an "O" in the author's note.
_____.**The Road to Oz.** Chicago: Reilly and Britton, 1909. First State has perfect type on pages 34 & 121 (broken in later states) with a number and caption in page 129.
_____.**The Patchwork Girl of Oz.** Chicago: Reilly and Britton, 1913. In the first state the "C" in "Chapter Three" is partially on page 35.
_____.**Tik-Tok of Oz.**

First Edition: Chicago: Reilly and Britton, 1914. Ads on verso of half title end with *The Patchwork Girl of Oz.*

_____.**The Scarecrow of Oz.**: Reilly and Britton, 1915. Ads on verso of half title end with *The Scarecrow of Oz.*

_____.**Rinkitink in Oz.** Chicago: Reilly and Britton, 1916. No ads in first issue.

_____.***The Lost Princess of Oz.*** Chicago: Reilly and Britton, 1904. Ads on verso of half title end with *The Lost Princess of Oz.*

N_____.**The Tin Woodsman of Oz.** Chicago: Reilly and Britton, 1918. Ads on verso of half title end with *The Tin Woodsman of Oz.*

_____.**The Magic of Oz.**: Reilly and Britton, 1919. Ads on verso of half title end with *The Tin Woodsman of Oz.*

_____. **The Wonderful Wizard of Oz.** Chicago and New York, Geo M. Hill, 1900. There are three states of the first edition. The true first is determined by a blank title page verso, two dark blotches on the moon in plate facing p. 34 and a red horizon/background in plate facing p. 92.

Beattie, Ann. **Secrets and Surprises**. NY: Random House, 1979. FIRST EDITION stated with number line "2 4 6 8 9 7 5 3".

Bechdolt, Frederick. **Tales of the Old Timers**. New York: The Century Co., 1924. Frontespiece by Fredrick Remington.

Beckett, Samuel. **Molloy.** Paris: Olympia Press, 1955. First issue has no price on rear flap.

Bellamy, Edward. **Looking Backward 2000-1887.** Boston: Ticknor and Company, 1888. "Press of J. J. Arakelyan" on verso in first printing.

Bellow, Saul. **The Adventures of Augie March.** NY: Viking, 1953. States "Published by the Viking Press, in September 1953"." No other printings stated.

_____. **Herzog.** NY: Viking, 1964. States "First published in 1964 by the Viking Press, Inc." No other printings stated. Verso states H. Wolf Book Manufacturing Co, Inc., and a line that says "M B G".

_____. **Humboldt's Gift.** NY: Viking, 1975. States "First published in 1975 by the Viking Press, Inc." No other printings stated.

_____. **Mr. Sammler's Planet.** NY: Viking, 1970. States "First published in 1970 by the Viking Press, Inc." No other printings stated.

Benchley, Peter. **The Deep.** Garden City, NY: Doubleday, 1974. First Edition is stated.

_____. **Jaws.** Garden City, NY. Doubleday, 1974. First Edition is stated, and 044 is printed on the last page.

Berendt, John. **Midnight in the Garden of Good and Evil**. NY: Knopf, 1994. "First Edition" is stated with number line "2 4 6 8 9 7 5 3". Dark green boards with black cloth spin. "fmr" on Page 11, line 32. 1st issue dust jacket price has Ann Beattie blurb at the top of the rear panel.

Berg, Elizabeth. **Open House**. NY: Random House, 2000. FIRST EDITION stated with number line "2 4 6 8 9 7 5 3".

Bierce, Ambrose. **Shapes of Clay**. San Francisco W.E. Wood 1903. Page 71 lines 5 and 6 read: "We've nothing better here than bliss. Walk in.But I must tell you this:".

Bissinger, H. G. **Friday Night Lights**. Reading, MA: Addison-Wesley Publishing, 1990. First printing, July 1990 is stated with number line "ABCDEFGHIJ-MW-943210".

Blank, Clair. **Beverly Gray at the World's Fair.** New York & Chicago A. L. Burt Company 1935. The front flap lists The Arden Blake Mystery Series by Cleo F. Garis. Back flap lists The Mary Lou Series by Edith Lovell.

Blatty, William Peter. **The Exorcist**. NY: Harper, 1971. FIRST EDITION is stated with "71 72 73 10 9 8 7 6 5 4 3 2 1" on the last page. 1st issue dust jacket has code "0571".

Bohjalan, Chris. **Midwives**. NY: Norton, 1969. First Edition stated with number line "10 9 8 7 6 5 4 3 2 1".
_____. **The Trans-Sister Radio**. NY: Harmony, 2000. First Edition stated with number line "10 9 8 7 6 5 4 3 2 1".

Boylan, Grace and Ike Morgan. **Kids of Many Colors. Volume One.** Chicago: Jamieson Higgins Co. 1901. Jamieson imprint & colophon dated 1901.

Bradbury, Ray. **Fahrenheit 451.** New York: Ballantine, 1953. PBO contains two short stories, The Playground & And the Rock Cried.

Bradley, Bill. **Time Present, Time Past.** NY: Knopf, 1996. First Edition is stated.

Braque, Georges. **Ten Works. With a Discussion by the Artist: Braque Speaks to Dora Vallier.** New York: Harcourt, Brace & World, 1963. Limited. First 35 with original signed lithograph 330 copies total.

Bromfield, Louis. **Early Autumn.** NY: Stokes, 1926. No statements of subsequent printings should be present on the copyright page.

Brooks, Geraldine. **March**. NY: Viking, 2005. Number line is - "1 3 5 7 9 10 8 6 4 2"

_____. **Year of Wonders**. NY: Viking, 2001. "First published in 2001 by Viking Penguin," stated with number line "1 3 5 7 9 10 8 6 4 2". Black boards with black spine. 1st issue dust jacket has five reviews.

Brown, Dan. **The DaVinci Code**. Garden City, NY: Doubleday, 2003. First Edition stated with the number line "10 9 8 7 6 5 4 3 2 1" Note Book Club edition replicates code and "First Edition", true first is 9.5" while BC is 8.5".

_____. **Digital Fortress**. NY: St. Martins, 1998. "First Edition: February 1998" stated with number line "10 9 8 7 6 5 4 3 2 1".

Buck, Pearl S. **The Good Earth**. NY: John Day, 1931. No mention of subsequent printings. The bottom of the verso states "FOR THE JOHN DAY PUBLISHING COMPANY, INC." later changed to "FOR THE JOHN DAY COMPANY" late into the first printing, and on all subsequent printings. Although the "JOHN DAY PUBLISHING COMPANY" error is the first state, the second state "JOHN DAY COMPANY" is more scarce.

Buckley, Christopher. **Thank You for Smoking.** NY: Random House, 1994. First Edition stated with number line "24689753".

Buckley, William F. Jr. **On the Firing Line.** Franklin Center, PA: Franklin Library, 1989. Franklin Library "Signed First Edition."

Burgess, Anthony. **A Clockwork Orange**. London: Heinemann, 1962. First Issue is black boards with silver lettering, the first state dust jacket carries an ad for Burgess' *Devil of a State* on rear panel.

Burnett, Francis Hodgeson. **Little Lord Fauntleroy.** New York: Scribners, 1886. First Issue has a Devinne Press seal p. 201 and "14" lower right margin on P.209.

Burroughs, Edgar Rice. **Tarzan of the Apes**. Chicago: A. C. McClurg & Co., 1914. First state has an acorn stamped between the A. and C. on the spine.

_____. **The Return of Tarzan**.: A. C. McClurg & Co. 1915. First Printing has W.F. Hall imprint on the copyright page.

_____. **Jungle Tales of Tarzan.** Chicago: A. C. McClurg & Co. 1919. First issue is bound in orange, subsequent issues in green.

_____. **The Gods of Mars**. Chicago: A. C. McClurg & Co. 1918. First Printing has W.F,Hall imprint on the copyright page.

Burroughs, William S. **Naked Lunch.** Paris: Olympia Press, 1959. A green paperback No. 79 in the Traveler's Companion Series. No dust jacket (added a month after publication). A green border on the title page. 1st U.S.Edition- New York: Grove Press, 1959. First issue dust jacket lacks publisher's zip code on rear panel.

Butler, Robert Olen. **A Good Scent from a Strange Mountain.** NY: Holt, 1992. Number line "1 3 5 7 9 10 8 6 4 2". 1st Issue dust jacket has "Ret:0392:001945:50" in bottom left corner.

Byatt, A.S. **Possession.** London: Chatto and Windus, 1990. "Published in 1990 by Chatto & Windus" stated as is printer Butler and Tanner. Blue boards with blue topstain and a sewn-in dark blue ribbon bookmark.

Campbell, John W. Jr. **Who goes There?** Chicago: Shasta Publishers, 1948. Colophon Page with unstated limitation marks the first issue.

Camus, Albert. **The Outsider.** London: Hamish Hamilton, 1946. Original dust jacket price is 6s. net.
_____. **Resistance, Rebellion, and Death.** London: Hamish Hamilton, 1961. First US Edition: New York: Alfred A. Knopf , 1961. The first state dustjacket lacks a Rolo quote on the front flap.

Capote, Truman. **Breakfast at Tiffany's.** NY: Random House, 1958. First Printing stated. Yellow cloth boards with gilt lettering on a black rectangle pattern on the spine, and with light gray top stain. 1st issue dust jacket carries code "10/58".
_____. **In Cold Blood.** NY: Random House, 1965. 500 copies of the first edition were specially bound and signed by Capote. In the first trade edition, "FIRST PRINTING" is stated with no book club mark on back of book, 1st issue dust jacket has price of $5.95 code "1/66".

Carnegie, Dale. **How to Win Friends and Influence People**. NY: Simon & Schuster, 1936. "1936" stated on title page, with no subsequent printings listed on verso, in red cloth. 1st issue dust jacket has testimonial by Lowell Thomas, and the front flap says "Chicago University".

Carroll, Lewis (Charles Dodgson). **Alice's Adventures in Wonderland.** London: Macmillan & Co., 1866. Red cloth binding with gilt titles to spine, circular gilt decoration to boards, powder blue endpapers, all edges gilt.
_____. **The Hunting of the Snark.** London: Macmillan, 1876. Limited: (20 in Dark Blue, 20 in White and 100 in Red for Presentation. First trade edition: London: Macmillan, 1876. Issued in Buff Cloth with black endpapers.

Carson, Rachel. **The Silent Spring**. Boston: Houghton Mifflin. 1962. FIRST PRINTING is stated.

Carter, Stephen L. **The Emperor of Ocean Park.** NY: Knopf, 2002. FIRST EDITION stated. Red Boards with a black spine. Book club edition also states FIRST EDITION, but is bound in black.

Cary, Joyce. **The Horse's Mouth.** London: Michael Joseph, 1944. First state dustjecket had "No. 7768" on front flap; "No. 7769"on the back flap, and "No. 3170" on the back panel.

Casey, John. **Spartina.** NY: Knopf, 1989. "First Edition" is stated. Quarter bound with teal paper boards and cream white cloth spine, and blue top stain. 1st issue dust jacket has reviews by Paul Theroux, Ann Beattie, and George Garrett.

Castro, Ferreira de. **Jungle: a Tale of the Amazon Rubber-Tappers.** New York: Viking Press, 1935. The Viking Edition is bound British sheets and the Knopf, also 1935 is sometimes considered the First US edition as it was printed in the U. S.

Cather, Willa. **One of Ours.** NY: Knopf, 1922. Limited edition of 345 large paper copies, signed by the author, 35 on Imperial Japan Vellum.

Chabon, Michael. **The Amazing Adventures of Kavalier and Clay**. NY: Random House, 2000. Boards are white paper with colored threads and "MC" embossed on the front. The spine is the same color but in cloth. Number line "2 4 6 8 9 7 5 3" with "FIRST EDITION". Back of first issue dust jacket has no reviews.
_____. **The Mysteries of Pittsburgh**. NY: Morrow, 1988. First Edition stated with number line "1 2 3 4 5 6 7 8 9 10". White boards with purple cloth spine and silver lettering. Page 280, line 21 where it says "gone to far" rather than "gone too far" in first two printings.
_____. **Summerland**. NY: Hyperion, 2002. First Edition stated with number line "10 9 8 7 6 5 4 3 2 1".

Chadwick, Lester. **Baseball Joe Captain of the Team.** New York: Cupples & Leon, 1924. First is Gray cloth with Blue lettering.
_____. **Baseball Joe Pitching Wizard.** New York: Cupples & Leon, 1928. First is Gray cloth with Blue lettering.

Chambers, Robert W. **The King In Yellow.** Chicago : F. Tennyson Neely 1895. First state is green cloth with no frontispiece.

Chandler, Raymond. **The Little Sister.**: Hamish Hamilton, 1949. First Issue is red cloth with gilt lettering.
_____. **The Long Good-Bye.** London: Hamish Hamilton, 1953. First Issue is gray cloth with orange lettering.

_____. **Playback.** London: Hamish Hamilton, 1958. First Issue is red cloth with silver lettering.

Cheever, John. **The Enormous Radio**. NY: Funk & Wagnalls, 1953. "I" on the verso, blue-green cloth stamped in gilt. 1st issue dust jacket carries no reviews.

_____. **The Falconer.** NY: Knopf, 1977. "First Edition" is stated.

_____. **The Stories of John Cheever.** NY: Knopf, 1978. "First Edition" is stated.

_____. **The Wapshot Chronicle.** NY: Harper, 1957. FIRST EDITION is stated and the Harper code is B-G, light blue cloth with black spine and gold letters. 1st issue dust jacket has blurbs by Jean Stafford, Francis Steegmuller, and Robert Penn Warren.

Chesterton, G.K. **The Scandal of Father Brown.** London: Cassell, 1935. Later Editions add the story "The Vampire of the Village."

Christie, Agatha. **Murder in the Mews.** London: Collins / Crime Club, 1937. First issue is blue boards with gilt lettering.

_____. **Death on the Nile.** London: Collins / Crime Club, 1937. First issue is brown cloth with black lettering, original dust jacket price is 7s. 6d.

_____. **The Hollow.** London: Collins / Crime Club, 1946. First issue is red boards with black lettering on spine, original dust jacket price is 8s. 6d. Net.

_____. **The Labors of Hercules.** London: Collins / Crime Club, 1947. First issue is orange cloth with black lettering on spine, original dust jacket price is 8s. 6d. Net.

_____. **Mrs McGinty's Dead.** London: Collins / Crime Club, 1952. First issue is red cloth with black lettering on spine.

_____. **After the Funeral.** London: Collins / Crime Club, 1953.First issue is green boards with black lettering.

_____. **The Clocks.** London: Collins / Crime Club, 1963. First issue is orange boards clocks with black lettering on spine.

_____. **4:50 from Paddington.** London: Collins / Crime Club, 1957. First issue is red cloth with black lettering on spine.

_____. **A Caribbean Mystery.** London: Collins / Crime Club, 1964. First issue is red cloth with gilt lettering on a bright red spine.

_____. **Nemesis.** London: Collins / Crime Club, 1971. First issue is red cloth with gilt Nemesis lettering on spine.

Clancy, Tom. **The Hunt for Red October.** Annapolis: Naval Institute Press, 1984. The verso has 18 lines of text and no statement of printing. 1st issue dust jacket has 6 review blurbs on the back in this order: Jack Higgins, Joseph Wambaugh, Clive Cussler, Edward L. Beach, John Moore, and Stansfield Turner.

_____. **Patriot Games**. NY: Putnam, 1986. Number line "1 2 3 4 5 6 7 8 9 10". Light gray boards with off-white cloth spine and gold lettering. 1st issue dust jacket has seven reviews.

_____. **Red Storm Rising**. NY: Putnam, 1986. Number line "1 2 3 4 5 6 7 8 9 10". Marbled black boards with navy blue cloth spine, and gold lettering.

Clinton, William. **Between Hope and History**. NY: Times Books/ Random House, 1996. FIRST EDITION is stated with 2 4 6 8 7 5 3 number line.

Condon, Richard. **The Manchurian Candidate.** NY: McGraw-Hill, 1959. First Edition stated. 1st issue dust jacket has price of $4.50 and no reviews.

Conrad, Joseph. **Lord Jim.** Edinburgh and London: Blackwood, 1900. Originally issued in green card covers with thistle gilt on spine. First Issue, "anyrate" in line 5 of p. 77; 7 lines from the bottom of p. 226, there is no "keep" after "can"; also in the seventh line from the bottom of p. 226, it is "cure" instead of "cured;" in the last line of p. 319, "his" is out of alignment.

Conroy, Pat. **The Boo**. Verona, VA: McClure Press, 1970. "First Printing" stated.

_____. **The Prince of Tides**. Boston: Houghton Mifflin, 1986. Number line "S 10 9 8 7 6 5 4 3 2 1".

Cooper James Fenimore. **Pathfinder; or, The Inland Sea.**(Two Volumes) Philadelphia: Lea & Blanchard, 1840. Second volume lacks a copyright notice in the first issue.

Cormier, Robert. **The Chocolate War.** New York: Pantheon, 1974. First issue is brown boards with gilt lettering on spine.

Coward, Noel. **Present Indicative.** London: William Heinemann Ltd., 1937. First issue has a wrap around band indicating a "Book Society Choice".

Cozzens, James Gould. **Guard of Honor.** NY: Harcourt, 1948. "first edition" is stated.

Crane, Hart. **White Buildings.** New York: Boni & Liveright, 1926. Allen Tate's name incorrectly on title page.

_____. **Collected Poems of Hart Crane.** New York: Liveright, 1933. The first state lacks a period following "Inc" on the title page.

Crane, Stephen. **Red Badge of Courage.** New York D. Appleton and Company 1895. In the first state page 225 has "congratulated" in unbroken type.

Crichton, Michael. **The Andromeda Strain**. NY: Knopf, 1969. "FIRST EDITION" is stated.

_____. **The Great Train Robbery**. NY: Knopf, 1969. "FIRST EDITION" is stated. Olive boards with maroon cloth spine and gold lettering and green top stain 1st issue dust jacket has ISBN on bottom right corner and no reviews.

_____. **Jurassic Park.** . Franklin Center, PA: Franklin Library, 1990. Franklin Library "Signed First Edition."

Crowley, Aleister. **Magick in Theory and Practice.** Paris: Lecram Press, 1929. "Published for Subscribers Only", with a dust Jacket and a colored plate of the sigil of "Master Theron."

_____. **Moonchild.** London: The Mandrake Press. 1929. First issue is green cloth with gilt lettering on spine.

cummings, e.e. **The Enormous Room.** Boni and Liveright: New York, 1922. First issue, the word "shit" intact in the last line of page 219. In later issues the word was blocked out.

Cunningham, Michael. **The Hours.** NY: Farrar, Strauss and Giroux, 1966. "First Edition" is stated, the spine section is brown and the rest of the book is tan.

Darrow, Clarence. **The Story of My Life.** New York: Charles Scribner's Sons, 1932. A limited edition of 294 numbered and signed copies with some unnumbered and signed copies apparently slipping by.

Davis, G. A. **Robin Hood.** Springfield, MA: McLoughlin Bros., 1929. First Edition is Die cut and Springfield, MA not New York.

Davis, Harold Lenoir. **Honey in the Horn.** NY: Harper, 1934. "First Edition" stated on the first printing with Harper code "M-I"

Davis, Richard Harding. **Gallegher and Other Stories.** New York: Scribners, 1891. First issue lacks an ad for "Famous Women of the French Court"

Delany, Samuel R. **Babel-17.** NY: ACE, 1966. PBO ACE F-388.

DeLillo. **White Noise.** NY: Viking, 1985. "First published in 1985 by Viking Penguin Inc." stated, gray boards with white cloth spine.

Dexter, Pete. **Paris Trout**. NY: Random House, 1988. First Edition stated with number line "9 8 7 6 5 4 3 2".

Dickey, James. **Deliverance**. Boston: Houghton Mifflin. 1970. First state of dust Jacket carries 6-84530 on rear flap.

DiDonato, Pietro. **Christ in Concrete.** NY: Esquire, 1937. First Edition is stated. Expanded version using Esquire version as first chapter is also titled **Christ in Concrete**. Indianapolis: Bobbs-Merrill, 1939. First Edition is stated.

Diaz, Junot. **The Brief Wonderous Life of Oscar Wao.** NY: Riverhead, 2007. Number line is "1 3 5 7 9 10 8 6 4 2". Boards are white with white cloth spine and red lettering. 1st Issue dust Jacket has 3 reviews - by Walter Mosley, *The New York Times Book Review*, and *Newsweek.*

Dick, Philip K. **A Handful of Darkness.** London: Rich & Cowen 1955. No listing of "World of Chance" on rear panel.
_____. **Flow My Tears the Policeman Said.** New York: Doubleday, 1974. Code O50 on page 231

Dixon, Franklin W. **The Tower Treasure.** New York: Grosset & Dunlap, 1927. First Hardy Boys book. Ads in Back starting with "This Isn't All!", Tom Swift Series 29 titles ending with Airline Express, Don Sturdy 7 titles ending Among Gorillas, Radio Boys Series, Garry Grayson Football Series, Ending with Western Stories For Boys with 5 titles Round-Up Being Last Title , in red cloth.

Dobie, J. Frank. **Coronado's Children.** Dallas, TX: The Southwest Press, 1930. First printing dedication is from "a cowman of the Texas soil. "
_____. **Mustangs**. Boston: Little, Brown, 1952. Bound in cowhide and issued in a slipcase.

Doctorow, E. L. **World's Fair.** NY: Random House, 1985. First Edition stated with number line "24689753, blue boards with gold lettering on spine. 1st issue dust jacket carries no reviews. 300 copies of the first edition were specially bound with signed limitation pages tipped in, and issued in slipcases.

Donleavy, J.P. **The Ginger Man.** Paris: Olympia Press, 1955. #7 in Traveler's Companion Series, Price on rear cover is "Francs 1,500"

Doyle, Arthur Conan. **The Adventures Of Sherlock Holmes.** London: George Newnes, 1892. The first issue has a blank street sign on the front cover.
_____. **The Memoirs Of Sherlock Holmes.** London: George Newnes, 1894. Blue beveled boards lettered in gilt decorated in black.
_____. **The Hound of the Baskervilles.** London: Georges Newnes, 1902. The first issue lacks a publication date on the verso.
_____. **The Return Of Sherlock Holmes.** London: Georges Newnes, 1905. "you" on page 3 line 3 in first issue.

Drury, Alan. **Advise and Consent.** Garden City, NY: Doubleday, 1959. First Edition" is stated on bottom of copyright page. 1st state dust jacket is priced $5.75 with a higher price blacked-out.

Durrell, Lawrence. **The Black Book.** Paris: The Obelisk Press, 1938. First U.S. Edition: New York: E. P. Dutton, 1960. First state dust jacket reads "Lawrence Durrel's Black Book" not "T. S. Eliot said…"
_____. **Justine.** London: Faber & Faber, 1957. First state dust jacket lacks review by Gerald Sykes on front flap.
_____. **Pied Piper of Lovers.** London: Cassell, 1935. Spine misprints title as 'Pied Pipers of Lovers' .

Eberhart, Richard. **A Bravery of Earth.** London: Cape, 1930. First State contains an errata slip.

Eddison, E.R. **The Worm Ouroboros.** London: Jonathan Cape, 1922. The first issue has a windmill blindstamped on the back cover.

Einstein, Albert. **The Evolution of Physics**. NY: Simon & Schuster, 1938. Title page and verso both state 1933 with no subsequent printings, simultaneous publication with Cambridge University Press in England and in Holland (by A. W. Sijthoff's Uitgeversmaatschappij.

Eisenhower, Dwight D. **Crusade in Europe**. Garden City, NY: Doubleday, 1948. A signed edition limited to one thousand four hundred and twenty-six numbered copies.

Eliot, George. **The Mill on the Floss.** (3 Vol. set). Edinburgh and London: William Blackwood 1860. Two Bindings A) original orange-brown cloth, with 16 pages of ads in volume three. No ad leaf in the front of volume one. B) light brown cloth with blindstamped covers and gilt titles to the spine. Priority unknown.

Eliot, T. S. **The Cocktail Party.** London: Faber and Faber, 1950. Misprint "here" for "her" on Page 29.
_____. **The Wasteland.** New York. Boni and Liveright. 1922 . "Mountain" correctly spelled on page 41.

Ellison, Ralph. **Invisible Man**. NY: Random House, 1952. FIRST PRINTING stated.

Emerson, Ralph Waldo. **Nature.** Boston: James Munroe and Company, 1836. First edition, first state, has P. 94 misnumbered 92.

Eugenides, Jeffrey. **Middlesex**. NY: Farrar, Strauss and Giroux, 2002. Number line is "1 3 5 7 9 10 8 6 4 2".

Faulkner, William. **A Fable**. NY: Random House, 1954. Numbered and signed limited edition of 1,000 copies. First trade edition has "First Printing" stated. 1st state dust jacket has "8/54" on the bottom of the front flap.

_____. **As I Lay Dying. New** York: Jonathan Cape/Harrison Smith , 1930. Initial "I" on page 11 misaligned.

_____. **Absalom, Absalom!** NY: Random House, 1936. Signed edition limited to 300 copies. The book has half green cloth over patterned boards and top edge gilt. First trade edition states 1936 on the title page and verso with no additional statements of printings. Black boards with red horizontal lines and gilt lettering.

_____. **Collected Stories.** NY: Random House, 1950. "FIRST PRINTING" is stated. The title page has blue highlights over the book title with gray cloth with blue top stain. The spine of the book has an error where there is a "The". First issue dust jacket lacks "The".

_____. **The Reivers.** NY: Random House, 1962. "FIRST PRINTING" is stated on the copyright page. 500 copies of the first edition were printed on special paper, specially bound, and issued with a glassine dust wrapper, signed and numbered.

_____. **Sanctuary.** New York: Jonathan Cape & Harrison Smith, 1931. First issue endpapers are gray printed in magenta.

_____. **The Sound and the Fury.** New York: Jonathan Cape & Harrison Smith, 1929. Humanity Uprooted is priced at $3.00 on first state Dust Jacket.

Ferber, Edna. **So Big.** Garden City, NY: Doubleday, Page, 1924. Two states of the first edition no priority. On the title page of State 1, the "Y" in DOUBLEDAY is directly below the "T" in GARDEN CITY. On the title page of State 2, the "Y" in DOUBLEDAY is directly below the "TY" in GARDEN CITY.

Fitzgerald, F. Scott. **The Beautiful and Damned.** NY: Scribner, 1922. First edition, lacking the Scribner's seal to the verso of the title page, first issue dustjacket with title in Black with White lettering.

_____. **The Great Gatsby.** NY: Scribner, 1925. First edition, first issue (chatter on p. 60/16, northern on p. 119/22, sick in tired on p. 205/9, and Union Street Station on p. 211/7).

_____. **Tales of the Jazz Age.** NY: Charles Scribner's Sons. 1922. "Published September, 1922" and Scribner's collophon on the verso, with "and" for "an" on p. 232, line 6.

_____. **Taps At Reveille.** New York: Scribners, 1935. Page 51, lines 29 – 30 "Oh, catch it – oh, catch it.."

Flavin, Martin. **Journey in the Dark**. NY: Harper's, 1943. "FIRST EDITION" is stated on copyright page.

Fleming, Ian. **Casino Royale.** London: Jonathan Cape, 1953. Black cloth with red heart vignette on upper cover and titles on the spine, in gun metal grey.

_____. **Moonraker.** London: Jonathan Cape, 1955. Page ten misprints shoot as "shoo" in the first state.

_____. **The Spy Who Loved Me.** London, Jonathan Cape, 1962. The first state has a line between e and m in "Fleming" on the title page.

Ford, Richard. **Independence Day.** NY: Knopf, 1995. Limited edition of 150 copies signed and numbered. The first trade edition states "FIRST EDITION". "with" is missing on page 289, line 21.

Fox, John. **The Little Shepherd of Kingdom Come.** New York: Scribners, 1903. The first State has "laugh" for lap page 61, line 14.

_____. **The Trail of the Lonesome Pine.** New York: Charles Scribner's Sons, 1908. First Issue has a Scribner's seal on the verso.

Franzen, Jonathon. **The Corrections**. NY: Farrar, Strauss and Giroux, 2001. First Edition, 2001 is stated on the verso with erratum slip to reverse reading of pages 430 & 431 is laid in.

Frazier, Charles. **Cold Mountain.** NY: Atlantic Monthly Press, 1997. Signed edition limited to 500 copies in a slipcase. First trade edition number line "10 9 8 7 6 5 4 3 2 1" misprint on p. 25, line 16 ("man-woman" instead of "madwoman")

Freeman, R. Austin. **The Singing Bone.** London: Hodder & Stoughton, 1912. A first issue has: p.3, risen space before `THE' in running title; p.4, antepenultimate line, `t' in `train' broken; p.19, risen furniture after last line; p.46, last line, extra full-stop after `head'; p.170, l.1, broken `n' in `man'; p.184, l.7, broken `m' in `mother'; p.226, l.23, `his' for `he'; p.231, l.5, question mark after `that' instead of an exclamation mark; p.235, l.5, `know' for `now'

Frost, Robert. **A Boy's Will.** London: David Nutt, 1913. Four binding states, possibly more Nutt's bankruptcy scattered cut and gathered copies, most ending up with Dunster House Bookshop in Cambridge, Mass. Bronze Pebbled and White Linen bindings are the most common.

Gaddis, William. **A Frolic of His Own.** NY: Poseidon Press, 1994. Number line "1 3 5 7 9 10 8 6 4 2"

_____. **J R**. NY: Knopf, 1975. States "FIRST EDITION" hard cover and soft cover issued simultaneously.

Gabaldon, Diana. **Outlander.** NY: Delacorte, 1991. July 1991 stated and number line "10 9 8 7 6 5 4 3 2 1".

Gates, Bill. **The Road Ahead.** NY: Viking, 1995. "First published in 1995 by Viking Penguin," is stated with the number line "10 9 8 7 6 5 4 3 2 1".

Gibson, William. **Neuromancer.** NY: Ace, 1984. PBO with "Ace

Original/July 1984" on the verso.

Gilchrist, Ellen. **Victory Over Japan**. Boston: Little Brown, 1984. FIRST EDITION is stated, light brown boards with dark brown spine and gold lettering. 1st issue dust jacket has three reviews - The London Times Literary Suppliment, The Washington Post, and Harper's.

Ginsberg, Allen. **Howl and Other Poems.** San Francisco: City Lights, 1956 . Pocket Poets Series: Number Four. Stapled black wrappers with white wraparound pastedown. Rear cover is priced at 75 cents (printed in blue), and the rear label contains twenty lines of publisher"s text and a misprint of a period instead of comma on line 18.
       _____. **Kaddish and Other Poems 1958-1960.** San Francisco: City Lights Books, 1961. PBO, Number 14 in the Pocket Poets Series. Publisher's ten line statement on rear cover relaced by a twenty-three line statement in later printings.

Gissing, George. **The Private Papers of Henry Ryecroft.** Westminster: Archibald Constable & Co., 1903. The first issue has 3 pages of ads following text.

Glasgow, Ellen. **In this Our Life.** NY: Harcourt, 1941. "First Edition" is stated.

Glass, Julia. **Three Junes**. NY: Pantheon, 2002. First Edition stated with number line "2 4 6 8 9 7 5 3 1". 1st issue dust jacket has blurbs by Richard Russo, John Casey, and Michael Cunningham.

Glover, Mary Baker. **Science and Health.** Boston: Christian Scientist Publishing Company, 1875. Note the name of the author, reprints are as by Mary Baker Eddy, the first issue contains an errata slip.

Gogol, Nikolai. **The Inspector-General**. First Edition of Arthur Sykes transaltion: London: Walter Scott, 1892. First State includes an errata slip.

Golden, Arthur. **Memoirs of a Geisha.** NY: Knopf, 1997. States "FIRST EDITION"

Grahame, Kenneth. **Wind in the Willows** . London: Methuen and Co., 1908. Blue cloth pictorially stamped and lettered in gilt within a single gilt rule border on front cover and pictorially stamped and lettered in gilt on spine. Top edge gilt, others uncut.

Grau, Shirley Ann. The Keepers of the House. NY: Knopf, 1964. "FIRST EDITION" is stated.

Graves, Robert. **Good-Bye To All That: An Autobiography**. London. Jonathan Cape. First Edition, 1929. The first state carries a poem by Sassoon Pp 341-343.

Greenaway, Kate. **Marigold Garden.** London & New York: George Routledge, 1885. Front and rear illustrations match in the first issue.
_____. **Mother Goose or Old Nursery Rhymes.** London George Routledge, 1881.Last line of p.18 ending in "bush", page number 38 printed upside down and p.47 last line ending in "boy"in the first state.

Greene, Graham. **A Sort of Life**. London: The Bodley Head, 1971. The first state has "Sir John Barrie" page 177, line 4.

Grey, Zane. **Wanderer of the Wasteland.** New York: Harper and Brothers, 1923. Code for the first issue is "L-W".

Grisham, John. **A Time to Kill.** NY: Wynwood Press, 1989. Subtitle "A Novel of Retribution" and the price on the front flap is $18.95.
_____**The Firm**. Garden City, NY: Doubleday, 1991. "First Edition" stated with "1 3 5 7 9 10 8 6 4 2" number line. The first state has light gray boards with black cloth spine, the second dark gray boards, the first state has precedence.

Gurdjieff, G. I. **Meetings with Remarkable Men**. NY: Dutton, 1963. First American edition states "First published in the U.S.A, 1963" and "Printed in Great Britain"with no subsequent printings listed and "Dutton" at the bottom of the spine. 1st issue dust jacket has "Dutton" on the spine and carries blurb by Frank Lloyd Wright.

Guthrie, A. Jr. **The Way West.** NY: William Sloane, 1949. "First Printing" is stated on the copyright page with no mention of the press that printed the book. Boards are battleship gray with a blue/green cloth spine. (Note: Book Club editions are close, check for detent and/or code "RD 7 W" on the last page).

Haggard, H. Rider. **King Solomon's Mines.** London, Cassell & Co. 1885. First Issue has 16 pages of ads at the rear dated 5 G.8.85 and 5 B 8.85; page 10 has the misprint Bamamgwato; page 122 has "to let twins to live"; page 307 has "until the new wrod supplants the old".
_____. **Allan Quatermain.** London: Longmans,Green & Co, 1887. In the first state "Qaurtermain" is mis-spelled on page 78.
_____. **She A History of Adventure.** London: Longmans, Green, and Co., 1887. The first Issue, has the following errors; 'geneleman' for 'gentleman' p.59, line 22, 'had' for 'have' p126, line 26, 'it compared' for 'if compared' p.258, line37 and 'godness me' p.269, line 38.

Hamsun, Knut. **Hunger.** London: Leonard Smithers, 1899. First printing announces Smither's "List of Publications" for Spring 1899.

Hardy, Thomas. **Tess of the d'Urbervilles: A Pure Woman Faithfully Presented.** London: James R. Osgood, McIlvaine, 1891.

(Three Volumes) Chapter XXV for 'Chapter XXXV on page 199 of volume 2.

Harris, Joel Chandler. **Uncle Remus His Songs & His Sayings**. New York : D. Appleton, 1881. The last line on page 9 "presumptive".

Harris, Thomas. **The Silence of the Lambs.** NY: St. Martins, 1988. "First Edition" stated with number line "10 9 8 7 6 5 4 3 2 1". Boards are gray with author's initials blind stamp and burgundy cloth spine.

Hassam, Childe **The Etchings and Dry-Points of Childe Hassam**. New York: Charles Scribner's Sons, 1925. In the first edition, the initial etching "Cos Cob" is signed.

Haven, Charles T. and Frank A. Belden. **A History of the Colt Revolver.** New York: William Morrow, 1940. A limited edition signed by both authors and the Sectretary and a Vice-President of the Colt Arms Co.

Hawking, Stephen. **A Brief History of Time**. London: Bantam, 1988. "Published 1988 by Bantam Press", and no statement of reprints. The first state of the U.S. first edition was withdrawn and lacks the table of contents and dedication statement. It has number line "0 9 8 7 6 5 4 3 2 1" and ISBN 0-553-05243-8 with a dust jacket that is silver. The second state of the U.S. first edition has number line "0 9 8 7 6 5 4 3 2 1" a dedication on the verso, a table of contents, an ISBN is 0-553-05340-X, and a blue dust jacket.

Hawthorne, Nathaniel. **The Scarlet Letter.** Boston: Ticknor, Reed & Fields, 1850. First State has a misprint "reduplicate" for "repudiate" at line 20 page 21.

Hazzard, Shirley. **The Great Fire**. Farrar, Strauss and Giroux, 2003. "FIRST EDITION, 2003" stated with number line "1 3 5 7 9 10 8 6 4 2". 1st issue dust jacket has reviews by Michael Cunningham, Joan Didion, and Ann Patchett.

Heckstall-Smith, Anthony. **The Consort.** London: Anthony Blond, 1962. First US Edition: New York: Grove Press, 1965. Issued with two Dust Jackets, one clothed one nude.

Heinneman, Larry. **Paco's Story**. Farrar, Strauss and Giroux, 1986. "FIRST EDITION, 1986" stated, orange boards with black cloth spine and gold lettering. First issue dust jacket carries Gloria Emerson, Tracy Kidder, and Robert Mason.

Heinlein, Robert A. **Stranger in a Strange Land.** New York: G. P. Putnam's, 1961. The first printing has a code C22 on page 408.

Heller, Joseph. **Catch 22**. NY: Simon & Schuster, 1961. FIRST PRINTING stated. 1st issue dust jacket is priced $5.95 with no blurbs.

Hemingway, Ernest. **A Farewell to Arms.** NY: Scribner, 1929. Limited to 510 signed copies issued in a slipcase. The first trade edition states 1929 on title page and the verso and the Scribner's seal and lacks a legal disclaimer found on later printings on page x. 1st issue dust jacket is priced $2.50 and has a misspelling - "Katherine Barclay" instead of "Catherine Barkley".

_____. **For Whom the Bell Tolls.** NY: Scribner, 1940. Two varients one with and "A" alone on the verso and one with an "A" and the Scribner collophon, no known precedence. 1st issue dust jacket lacks a credit under photo of Hemingway.

_____. **The Old Man and The Sea.** NY: Scribner, 1952. Copyright page bears the letter "A" and the Scribner's colophon.

_____. **The Sun also Rises.** NY: Scribner, 1926. The first edition, first issue, with "stoppped" on page 181, line 26 in the first issue dust jacket with the misprint on the front panel ("In Our Times" vs. "In Our Time").

Herbert, Frank. **Dune,** Philadelphia: Chilton, 1965. First Edition stated with no mention of subsequent printings and no ISBN. First issue boards are blue with white lettering on the spine, and gray end papers. 1st issue dust jacket flap has four lines of publisher identification on the bottom beginning with "CHILTON BOOKS".

Henry, O. **Postscripts**. New York: Harper & Brothers, 1923. The first state is red cloth stamped in gilt.

Hersey, John. **A Bell for Adano.** NY: Knopf, 1944. "First Edition" is stated.

_____. **Hiroshima**. NY: Knopf, 1944. "First Edition" is stated with blue and green boards no known priority.

Hijuelos, Oscar. **The mambo kings play songs of love.** NY: Farrar, Strauss and Giroux, 1989. "FIRST EDITION, 1989" stated. Bound in orange cloth with two gold crowns on the front, and gold lettering on the spine. 1st Issue dust jacket has five reviews for *Our House in the Last World* the author's first novel.

Hildenbrand, Laura. **Seabiscuit.** NY: Random House, 2001. First Edition is stated with 24689753 number line black boards with black cloth spine and gold lettering. 1st issue dust jacket has no reference to audio book on the back flap.

Hofstadter, Douglas R. **Godel, Escher, Bach**. NY: Basic Books, 1979. Has the number line 10 9 8 7 6 5 4 3 2 1.

Holmes, Oliver Wendell. **The Common Law.** Boston: Little, Brown, and Company, 1881. Original is bound in russet cloth.

Hoover, Herbert. **A Challenge to Liberty.** NY: Scribner, 1934. has an "A" and the Scribner colophon (seal). Issued with red and blue boards no known priority.

Howard, Robert E. **Always Comes Evening.** Sauk City, WI: Arkham House, 1957. Compiled by Glenn Lord. Published by Arkham House, subsidized by Lord. 636 copies printed. The first 536 copies were imprinted on the spine with the lettering running bottom to top, European style, the final 100 copies were imprinted top to bottom, American style.

Hudson, W. H. **A Crystal Age.** London: T. Fisher Unwin, 1887. Author's name missing from the title page in the first issue.

Huxley, Aldous. **Brave New World.** London; Chatto & Windus; 1932. Limited Edition of 324 Copies. First trade edition: London; Chatto & Windus; 1932. First issue is blue boards with gilt title on the spine and a blue topstain.

Irving, John. **The World According to Garp.** NY: Dutton, 1978. FIRST EDITION stated with the number line "10 9 8 7 6 5 4 3 2 1" 1st issue dust jacket carries a price of $10.95 and the code "0478".

James, Henry. **Daisy Miller: A Comedy In Three Acts.** Boston: James R Osgood & Co, 1883. First hardcover issue binding with James R. Osgood colophon on spine.

James, Will. **Smoky.** New York. Charles Scribners, 1929. First Issue has "Sand" as top title opposite title- page.

Jin, Ha. Waiting. New York: Pantheon, 1999. First Edition stated with number line "2 4 6 8 9 7 5 3 1".

Johnson, Charles. Middle Passage. NY: Atheneum, 1990. Number line "10 9 8 7 6 5 4 3 2 1". 1st issue dust jacket has blurbs by David Bradley, and Stanley Crouch.

Johnson, Denis. **Tree of Smoke.** NY: Farrar, Strauss and Giroux, 2007. "First edition, 2007" stated, number line is " 1 3 5 7 9 10 8 6 4 2"in mustard colored cloth. 1st issue dust jacket carries Jonathan Franzen, Chris Offutt, Philip Roth, David Gates, and Vince Passaro

Johnson, Josephine. **Now in November.** NY: Simon & Schuster, 1934. Both title page and verso state 1934. No printing statement.

Jones, Edward P. **The Known World.** NY: Amistad, 2003. Number line is "10 9 8 7 6 5 4 3 2 1".

Jones, James. **From Here to Eternity.** NY: Scribner, 1951. Limited edition with an extra page tipped in for a signature. First trade edition with the A and Scribner colophon on the copyright page. 1st issue dust jacket has a photo of the author with no reviews.

Joyce, James. **Ulysses.** Paris: Shakespeare & Co., 1922. First state issued in turquoise (blue/green) wraps.

Kahn, Roger. **The Boys of Summer.** NY: Harper, 1972. FIRST EDITION is stated with number line on the bottom of page 442 "72 73 74 75 10 9 8 7 6 5 4 3 2 1". Bound in beige and silver cloth with silver titles to the spine.

Kantor, MacKinlay. **Andersonville.** Cleveland and New York: World Publishing Company, 1955. Numbered and signed limited edition of 1,000 copies. First trade edition has "FIRST EDITION" stated.

Keene, Carolyn. **The Secret of Shadow Ranch.** Grosset and Dunlap: New York, 1931. First Issue has copyright page listing to this title and front flap of dust jacket listing to *The Secret of Red Gate Farm*.

Kennedy, John F. **Profiles in Courage.** NY: Harper's, 1955. States FIRST EDITION and M-E (December 1955).

Kennedy, Robert F. **The Enemy Within.** NY: Harper, 1960. FIRST EDITION is stated with Harper code A-K.
_____. **Thirteen Days**. NY: Norton, 1969. "First Edition January 20, 1969" is stated with number line "1 2 3 4 5 6 7 8 9 0". Caption on page 133 says Townley Smith instead of Bromley Smith. Caption on page 138 says Sorenson. Includes an errata slip.

Kennedy, William. **Ironweed.** NY: Viking, 1983. "First published in 1983 by The Viking Press" is with no other statements of subsequent printings, The misspelling of "perceivced" vs. "perceived" on page 205, line 22 (through third printing). 1st state dust jacket lacks author's picture.

Kenton, Maxwell. (Terry Southern and Mason Hoffenberg). **Candy.** Paris: Olympia Press, 1958. Both volumes printed: "Printed October 1958 by S.I.P. Montreuil, France"

Kerouac, Jack. **Mexico City Blues.** New York: Grove Press, Inc., 1959. Gray cloth, white pictorial dust-jacket, printed in black, design by Roy Kuhlman, author's photograph to rear panel, by William Eichel.
_____. **On the Road.** NY: Viking, 1957. "PUBLISHED IN 1957 BY THE VIKING PRESS, INC." and "PRINTED IN U.S.A. BY THE COLONIAL PRESS INC." stated with no other references to subsequent printings.

Kesey, Ken. **One Flew Over the Cuckoo's Nest. Dragon's Teeth**.

NY: Viking, 1962. "Published in 1962 by the Viking Press" stated. Misprints "that fool Red Cross woman" on page 9, lines 12-13; and "Red Cross woman named Gwen-doe-lin, with the blond hair the patients are always arguing about..." on the top of page 86. 1st issue dust Jacket has price of "$4.95" and a five-word Jack Kerouac blurb.

Kilmer, Joyce. **Trees and Other Poems.** New York: George H. Doran, 1914. Lacks "Printed in the U.S.A." on the verso, used in later printings.

King Stephen. **Carrie**. Garden City, NY: Doubleday, 1974. First Edition is stated, and "P6" is printed in the gutter on page 199.
_____. **Danse Macabre.** NY: Everest House, 1981. Edition of 250, 15 signed lettered copies. Code RRD281 on the verso.
_____. **The Dead Zone.** NY: Viking, 1979. "First Published in 1979 by the Viking Press" stated.
_____. **Firestarter**. NY: Viking, 1980. "First Published in 1980 by the Viking Press" stated. 1st issue dust jacket code is "0980".
_____. **Night Shift**. Garden City, NY: Doubleday, 1978. First Edition is stated, and "S52" is printed in the gutter on page 336.
_____. **The Shining**. Garden City, NY: Doubleday, 1977. First Edition is stated, and "R49" is printed in the gutter on page 447.
_____. **The Stand**. Garden City, NY: Doubleday, 1978. First Edition is stated, and "T39" is printed in the gutter on page 823.

Knox, Dudley W. **Naval Sketches of the War in California.** New York Random House 1939. Limited to 1000 copies printed by Grabhorn Press.

Kosinski, Jerzy. **Steps**. NY: Random House, 1968. "FIRST PRINTING" is stated, beige boards with maroon cloth spine and orange top stain. 1st issue dust jacket has six reviews for *The Painted Bird* beginning with Arthur Miller.

Lafarge, Oliver. **Laughing Boy.** Boston: Houghton Mifflin, 1929. The title page date must match the copyright date (1929).

Lahiri, Jhumpa. **Interpreter of Maladies**. Boston: Houghton Mifflin, 1999. PBO numberline "10 9 8 7 6 5 4 3 2 1". Title page states 1999

Lee, Harper. **To Kill a Mockingbird**. Philadelphia and New York, Lippincott, 1960. "FIRST EDITION" is stated. Two states of the first edition dust jacket. One state has two reviews on the back flap - by Shirley Ann Grau and Phyllis McGinley. The other state dust jacket has a single Jonathan Daniels review no known priority.

LeGuin, Ursula. **A Wizard of Earthsea.** Berkeley: Parnassus Press, 1968. Embossed cover with a smudge printed on
the title page. First State DJ had two prices, an "$3.95" in
the upper right hand corner of the front flap and

"Library Edition $3.90"

Lessing, Doris. **The Grass is Singing.** London, Michael Joseph. 1950. First issue has a band over the Dust Jacket Advertising that the book was a Daily Graphic pick of the month.

Lewis, Sinclair. **Arrowsmith.** NY: Harcourt, 1925. A limited edition signed, numbered and limited to 500 copies. Issued quarter bound in white buckram and blue boards with paper spine label, top edges gilt in a blue cardboard slipcase.
_____. **Elmer Gantry.** New York: Harcourt Brace, 1927. The spine of the first state substitutes a "C" for the "G" in "Gantry".

Lindberg, Charles. **The Spirit of St. Louis.** NY: Scribner, 1953. A signed and numbered presentation edition. The first trade edition has the verso "Printed in the United States of America" followed by "[A]", book club editions with the A are stated as printed by the Kingsport Press.

Lobeck, A. K. **Airways of America.** New York: Geographical Press, 1933. Title page and verso both state 1933 with no subsequent printings, a large fold-out map in rear pocket of book.

Lurie, Alison. **Foreign Affairs.** Franklin Center, PA: Franklin Library, 1984. Franklin Library "Signed First Edition."

MacDonald, John D. **The Deep Blue Good-by.** Greenwich, CT: Fawcett Publications, Inc., 1964. Paperback original Fawcett Gold Medal k1405
_____. **Nightmare in Pink .** Greenwich, CT: Fawcett Publications, Inc., 1964. Paperback original Fawcett Gold Medal k1406
_____. **A Purple Place for Dying .** Greenwich, CT: Fawcett Publications, Inc., 1964. Paperback original Fawcett Gold Medal k1417
_____. **The Quick Red Fox .** Greenwich, CT: Fawcett Publications, Inc., 1964. Paperback original Fawcett Gold Medal k1464
_____. **A Deadly Shade of Gold .** Greenwich, CT: Fawcett Publications, Inc., 1965. Paperback original Fawcett Gold Medal d1499
_____. **Bright Orange for the Shroud .** Greenwich, CT: Fawcett Publications, Inc., 1965. Paperback original Fawcett Gold Medal d1573
_____. **Darker than Amber.** Greenwich, CT: Fawcett Publications, Inc., 1966. Paperback original Fawcett Gold Medal d1674
_____. **One Fearful Yellow Eye .** Greenwich, CT: Fawcett Publications, Inc., 1966. Paperback original Fawcett Gold Medal d1759
_____. **Pale Gray for Guilt.** Greenwich, CT: Fawcett Publications, Inc., 1968. Paperback original Fawcett Gold Medal d1893
_____. **The Girl in the Plain Brown Wrapper.**

Greenwich, CT: Fawcett Publications, Inc., 1968. Paperback original Fawcett Gold Medal t2023

_____. **Dress Her in Indigo**. CT: Fawcett Publications, Inc., 1969. Paperback original Fawcett Gold Medal t2127

_____. **The Long Lavender Look.** Greenwich, CT: Fawcett Publications, Inc., 1969. Paperback original Fawcett Gold Medal m2325

_____. **A Tan and Shady Silence**. Greenwich, CT: Fawcett Publications, Inc., 1972. Paperback original Fawcett Gold Medal m2513

_____. **The Scarlet Ruse.** Greenwich, CT: Fawcett Publications, Inc., 1973. Paperback original Fawcett Gold Medal p2744

Mailer, Norman. **The Executioner's Song.** Boston: Little Brown, 1979. "FIRST EDITION" is stated.

_____. **The Naked and the Dead.** NY: Rinehart, 1948. Rinehart collophon is on the verso. 1st issue dust jacket has a review by Stanley Rinehart that begins on the front flap and continues on the back flap.

Malamud, Bernard. **The Fixer**. NY: Farrar, Strauss and Giroux, 1966. "First printing, 1966" is stated with yellow topstain.

_____. **The Magic Barrel. NY**: Farrar, Strauss and Cudahy, 1958. FIRST PRINTING, 1958 stated, boards are pink with illustration of yellow and purple chair and pale purple cloth spine with dark purple lettering. Jewish Publication Society of America edition is similarly marked with JPS as the publisher. 1st issue dust jacket has reviews for *The Assistant*.

_____. **The Natural.** NY: Harcourt, 1952. "first edition" stated. Three biding variants red, blue, and gray boards no known priority.

Marquand, John P. **The Late George Apley**. Boston: Little Brown, 1937. "Lovely Pearl" instead of "Pretty Pearl" on line 1 of page 19.

Marquez, Gabriel Garcia. **One Hundred Years of Solitude.** New York: Harper and Row, 1970. The first state of the Dust Jacket has a "!" at the end of the first paragraph on the front flap.

Marric, J. J. **Gideon's Fire.** New York: Harper, 1961. "First Edition" is stated with the Harper code "M-K"

Matthiessen, Peter. **Shadow Country.** NY: Modern Library Edition. 2008. Number line "2 4 6 8 9 7 5 3 1". Gray cloth with gold lettering. 1st issue dust jacket has front flap blurb by Don DeLillo and eight quotes on the back.

McCarthy, Cormac. **All the Pretty Horses**. NY: Knopf, 1992. Signed edition limited to 200 copies. First trade edition "First Edition" is stated. 1st state dust jacket the "A" in "All the Pretty Horses" is black.

_____. **Blood Meridian.** NY" Random House, 1985.
First Edition stated below number line "24689753". Red cloth spine
with gilt titles. Dust jacket back has code "394-54482-X".
_____. **The Road.** NY: Knopf, 2006 "First Edition" is
stated. 1st Issue dust jacket has $24.00 price.

McCullers, Carson. **The Heart is a Lonely Hunter.** Boston: Houghton
Mifflin, 1940. 1940 stated on both title page and verso. 1st state dust
jacket has a review of *Summer's Lease* by E. Arnot Robertson.

McCullogh, Colleen. **The Thorn Birds**. NY: Harper, 1977. FIRST
EDITION stated with number line 77 78 79 80 81 10 9 8 7 6 5 4 3 2 1.
1st issue dust jacket has price of $9.95 and the code "0577".

McCutcheon, George Barr . **Cowardice Court.** New York: Dodd,
Mead & Company, 1906. The spine in first issue splits the word
"Coward/Ice".
_____. **Graustark: The Story of a Love
Behind a Throne.** Chicago: Herbert S. Stone and Company, 1901.
Page 150, line 6 reads "Noble's".
_____. **Beverly of Graustark**. New York:
Dodd, Mead, 1904. Title page reads *"Harris N Fisher"*.

McDermott, Alice. **Charming Billy.** NY: Farrar, Strauss and Giroux,
1998. "First edition, 1998" stated.

McEwan, Ian. **Atonement**. London: Cape, 2001. Number line "2 4 6 8
10 9 7 5 3 1".

McFee, William. **Command.** Garden City, NY: Doubleday Page, 1922.
Page 185, line 31 reads "through thim" in first state.

McMurtry, Larry. **Lonesome Dove.** NY: Simon & Schuster, 1985. "10
9 8 7 6 5 4 3 2 1" on the verso, "he had none nothing" on page 621 line
16 (continues in some later printings).
_____. **Terms of Endearment.** NY: Simon & Schuster, 1975. "
"1 2 3 4 5 6 7 8 9 10"on the verso, tan paper boards with brown cloth
spine.

McPherson, James Alan. **Elbow Room.** Boston: Little Brown, 1977.
"FIRST EDITION" is stated. 1st state dust jacket has a single blurb by
Ralph Ellison.

Mencken, H. L. **The Philosophy Of Friedrich Neitzsche.** Boston:
Luce and Company, 1908. Spine reads "Philosophy of Neitzsche" in
first issue.

Merwin, W. S. **A Mask For Janus.** New Haven: Yale University
Press, 1952. Errata slip tipped-in at page 34.

Milar, Margaret. **Beast in View.** NY: Random House, 1955. First Printing stated.

Miller, Arthur. **Death of a Salesman.** NY: Viking, 1949. " PUBLISHED BY THE VIKING PRESS INC. IN March 1949" and "PRINTED IN U.S.A. BY AMERICAN BOOK-STRATFORD PRESS, INC., NEW YORK" stated. 1st issue dust jacket has the author's picture on the back flap, and the "S" in "SALESMAN" touches the arm of the salesman illustrated on the front.

Miller, Caroline. **Lamb in his Bosom.** NY: Harper, 1933. "First Edition" and H-H (August 1933) on copyright page.

Miller, Henry. **Tropic of Cancer.**: The Obelisk Press, 1934. Wrap around band "First Published September 1934" present for first issue.
_____. **Tropic of Capricorn.** Paris: Obelisk Press, 1939. Errata slip, and price (60 francs) stamped on back, in red wrappers lettered in black.

Miller, Walter M., Jr. **A Canticle for Leibowitz.** Philadelphia & NY: J. B. Lippincott Company, 1960. First state has a wrap around orange band with an endorsement from Ray Bradbury.

Millhauser, Steven. **Martin Dressler: The Tale of an American Dreamer.** NY: Crown, 1996. "First Edition" stated number line "10 9 8 7 6 5 4 3 2 1".

Milne, A.A. **When We Were Very Young.** London: Methuen & Co., 1924. Page ix is not numbered in the first issue.

Mitchell, Margaret. **Gone with the Wind.** NY: Macmillan, 1936. The verso states "Published May, 1936" with no other printing statements.

Mitchner, James A. **Tales of the South Pacific.** NY: Macmillan, 1947. "First Printing" is stated on the top of the copyright page. Printed by "THE VAIL-BALLOU PRESS INC." is stated on the bottom of the copyright page. Book is bound in orange-beige cloth, with letters on spine stamped in blue and no design on the front.

Momaday, N. Scott. **House Made of Dawn.** NY: Harper and Row, 1968. "FIRST EDITION" is stated.

Morley, Christopher. **Seacoast of Bohemia.** Garden City, NY: Doubleday Doran for the Old Realto Theater, 1929
Limited Edition of 50 Copies. Contains a postcard signed by Morley.
First trade edition: Garden City, NY: Doubleday Doran, 1929. Page 20, line 19 reads "rarely" in first state.

Moore, Robin. **The French Connection.** Boston: Little Brown, 1969. FIRST EDITION is stated.

Morris, William. **The Life and Death of Jason.** Hammersmith: Kelmscott Press, 1895. Printed in red and black, with two full-page illustrations by Edward Burne-Jones and initials and decorations by Morris. Bound in limp vellum with ribbon ties.

Morris, Wright. **The Field of Vision.** NY: Harcourt, 1956. "first edition" is stated, dark gray cloth with white circle pattern on the front, and red circle pattern on the spine. 1st issue jacket has black and blue printing.

Morrison, Toni. **Beloved.** NY: Knopf 1987. "First Edition" is stated.

Mundy, Talbot. **King of the Khyber Rifles.** Indianapolis IN: Bobbs-Merrill, 1916. In the first state the author's names is misspelled "Talbott" on the title page.

Nabokov, Valdimir. **Lolita.** Paris: Olympia Press, 1955. Two volume green PBO priced at 900 francs.

Nasar, Sylvia. **A Beautiful Mind.** NY: Simon & Schuster, 1998. Has the number line 10 9 8 7 6 5 4 3 2 1.

Nathan, Robert. *Portrait of Jennie.*: New York: Alfred A. Knopf, 1940. First state has "Stuart" page 29, line 5 and "onght" page 171, line 14.

Negroponte, Nicholas. **Being Digital**. New York: Alfred A. Knopf, 1995. First Edition is stated.

Nesbit, E. **The Railway Children.** London: Wells Gardner, Darton & Co. Ltd. 1906. First edition has gilt pictorial burgundy covers.

Nixon, Richard. **Six Crises.** Garden City, NY: Doubleday, 1962. First Edition is stated

Norris, Frank. **McTeague, A Story of San Francisco.** Garden City, NY: Doubleday & McClure, 1899.
First state has "moment" as last word on page 106.

Oates, Joyce Carol. **Them.** New York: Vanguard, 1969. No statements of additional printings, gray cloth with yellow top stain. 1st issue dust jacket is gray. Photo of author on the back of dust jacket is taken indoors, and author is looking to her left (toward spine), photo credit lacks "Black Star" has reviews by Publishers' Weekly and The Kirkus Reviews and a $6.95 price.

O'Connor, Edwin. **The Edge of Sadness.** Boston: Little Brown, 1961. "FIRST EDITION" is stated. However book club editions also carry the statement, check for detent (blind stamp) on rear board.

O'Hara, John. **Appointment in Samarra.** New York. Harcourt, Brace and Co. 1934. Errata slip tipped it to first issue.
_____. **Ten North Frederick.** NY: Random House, 1955. "FIRST PRINTING" is stated.

Orwell, George. **Animal Farm.** London, Secker & Warburg, 1945. First U.S. Edition: New York: Harcourt, Brace and Co. 1946. First issue dust jacket lacks "Published in the U.S.A." on rear flap.
_____. **1984.** London: Secker & Warburg, 1949. First Issue is green cloth with red lettering. There are two dust jackets, green and red, no known priority both priced 10s. net.
First US Edition: New York: Harcourt Brace, 1949. First Issue is gray boards red and black lettering. The dust jacket is priced "$3.00" with no book club slug.

Percy, Walker. **The Moviegoer.** NY: Knopf, 1961. "First Edition" is stated.1st issue dust jacket has code "0561", and no reviews.

Peterkin, Julia. **Scarlet Sister Mary.** Indianapolis: Bobbs-Merrill, 1928. "First Edition" is stated on the copyright page, limited signed editions that have an airplane on the front board were produced after the first edition.

Philbrick. Nathaniel. **In the Heart of the Sea**. NY Viking. 2000. "First published in 2000 by Viking Penguin," is stated with number line "1 3 5 7 9 10 8 6 4 2". 1st issue dust jacket has three reviews by Sebastian Junger, Richard Ellis, and Peter Benchley.

Poole, Ernest. **His Family.** NY: Macmillan, 1917. Date on title page and copyright page are both 1917.

Potter, Beatrix. **The Tale of Peter Rabbit.** London : Privately printed for the author by Strangeways, London, 1901. The first print run was 250 copies designated by the 1901 date, the second run was 1902.

Pound, Ezra. **Pavannes and Divisions.** New York: Alfred A. Knopf, 1918. The first issue is bound in dark blue cloth blindstamped with gilt on the spine.
_____. **Imaginary Letters.** Paris: Black Sun Press, 1930. Printed on Navarre Paper.

Powers. J. F. **Morte d'Urban**. Garden City, NY: Doubleday, 1962. "FIRST EDITION" is stated.

Powers, Richard. **The Echo Maker.** NY: Farrar, Strauss and Giroux, 2006. "First edition, 2006" stated, number line is " 1 3 5 7 9 10 8 6 4

2".

Prather, Richard S. **Kill The Clown.** Greenwich, CT: Fawcett, 1962. Paperback original Fawcett Gold Medal #s1208

Preston, Richard. **The Hot Zone**. NY: Random House, 1994. First Edition stated with number line "9 8 7 6 5 4 3 2".

Proulx, Annie. **The Shipping News**. NY: Scribner, 1993. Number line "10 9 8 7 6 5 4 3 2 1".

Pynchon, Thomas. **Gravity's Rainbow**. NY: Viking, 1973. "First published in 1973 in a hardbound and paperbound edition by The Viking Press, Inc., 625 Madison Avenue" a simultaneous issue both states are first editions. 1st issue dust jacket is priced $15. and carries code "0273".

Quaife, M. M. **Chicago's Highways Old & New: from Indian Trail to Motor Road.** Chicago: D.F. Keller & Company, 1923. Two fold out maps tipped in.

Rand, Ayn. **The Fountainhead.** Indianapolis: Boos-Merrill, 1943. First Edition is stated. 1st issue dust jacket carries a two column listing of other books published by Bobbs-Merrill.

Rawlings, Marjorie Kinnan. **The Yearling**. NY: Scribner's, 1938. The first printing has the letter "A" and Scribner's seal on the copyright page.

Remington, Frederic. **Done in the Open.** New York: R. H. Russell, Publisher, 1902. Signed, limited edition; with an introduction and verses by Owen Wister.

Rexroth, Kenneth. *In What Hour.* New York: Macmillan, 1940. Contains errata slip.

Richter, Conrad. **The Town**. NY: Knopf, 1950. "FIRST EDITION" is stated.
_____. **The Waters of Kronos.** NY: Knopf, 1960. "FIRST EDITION" is stated.

Riley, James Whitcomb. **Child-World.** Indianapolis, Bowen-Merrill, 1897. First Issue has a misprint on page ix "Proem".

Rinehart, Mary Roberts. **The Circular Staircase.** Indianapolis: Bobbs-Merrill, 1908. Issued in olive green cloth with orange lettering on front & spine and illustration of black spiral staircase on the cover. The dust jacket illustration features a full color image of a lady in nightgown with candlestick in hand fearfully descending a spiral staircase. The first edition includes a color frontispiece [with tissue guard] plus five black & white interior illustrations by Lester Ralph

Robinson, Edwin Arlington. **Tristram.** New York Macmillan 1927. First issue has "rocks" for "rooks" on p 86.

Robinson, Marilynne. **Gilead.** NY: Farrar, Strauss and Giroux, 2004. "First edition, 2004" stated, number line is "10 9 8 7 6 5 4 3 2 1". Simultaneous with Canadian edition Toronto: HarperCollins, 2004. Stated "First Canadian Edition". The publication date for both is November 4, 2004.

Roosevelt, Franklin. **On Our Way.** NY: John Day, 1934. COPYRIGHT, 1934, BY FRANKLIN D. ROOSEVELT on verso with 1 on bottom next to the publisher's device. The first state has party instead of property on page x, line 13; willing instead of unwilling on page 162, line 10. 1st issue dust jacket has photo of Roosevelt on the back with no revews

Roth, Philip. **American Pastoral.** Franklin Center, PA: Franklin Library, 1988. Franklin Library "Signed First Edition."
_____. **Sabbath's Theater.** Boston: Houghton Mifflin, 1995. Number line "MP 10 9 8 7 6 5 4 3 2 1". 1st issue dust jacket has no blurbs.

Rowling, J.K. **Harry Potter and the Philosopher's Stone.** London: Bloomsbury, 1997. The first state was issued without a dust jacket and the copyright credits "Joanne Rowling"
_____. **Harry Potter and the Chamber of Secrets.** London: Bloomsbury, 1998. The first state was issued without a dust jacket.
_____. **Harry Potter and the Prisoner of Azkaban.** London: Bloomsbury, 1999. The first state shows 'Copyright Joanne Rowling' on the copyright page. Clays Ltd is listed as the printer. The first page of text (page 7) has a misaligned dropped text block "burnt/so much". The second state has "J K Rowling" listed as copyright holder. Clays Ltd is also still noted as the printer. The dropped text on page 7 has been corrected. The third state lists J K Rowling as the copyright holder, and has the corrected text on page 7. It also has an added 2 pages of black and white advertisements for the first 2 books at the back of the book. And it lacks the Clays Ltd imprint, and lists no firm as the printer.
_____. **Harry Potter and the Order of the Phoenix**. London: Bloomsbury, 2003. On page 7 "The only person left outside was a teenage bo". Probably first state, but the publisher doesn't admit a priority.

Rush, Norman. **Mating.** . NY: Knopf, 1991. "First Edition" is stated.

Russell, Charles M. **Good Medicine.** . Garden City, NY: Doubleday, Doran & Co. 1929. Limited edition of 134 copies introduction by Will Rogers.

Russo, Richard. **Empire Falls.** NY: Knopf, 2001. "First Edition" is stated. Photo of the author on the back of 1st Issue dust jacket with two reviews - *Houston Chronicle* and Annie Proulx.

Salinger, J. D. **Catcher in the Rye**. Boston: Little Brown, 1951. FIRST EDITION is stated. 1st dust issue jacket has Salinger's black-and-white photograph portrait credited to Lotte Jacobi.

Samuels, Ernest . **Henry Adams.** Cambridge, MA: Belknap Press of Harvard University, 1965. Three volumes issued in a slipcase.

Sandburg, Carl. **Cornhuskers**. New York: Henry Holt and Co., 1918. In the first issue the price for *Chicago Poems* in the list opposite the title page is "$1.30".

Settle, Mary Lee. **Blood Tie.** Boston: Houghton Mifflin, 1977. Number line "S 10 9 8 7 6 5 4 3 2 1". 1st issue dust jacket has blurbs by Vance Bourjaily, Ann Beattie, and Douglas Day.

Seuss, Dr. **Bartholomew and the Oobleck.** New York: Random House, 1949. First printing had blue covers and dust jacket, later printings were in red. 1st issue dust jacket price is 200/200, flaps are white with black text.
_____. **The Cat In The Hat.** New York: Random House, 1957. The first state has matte boards.
_____. **The Eye Book.** New York: Random House, 1968. 1st issue dust jacket has 195/195 on the front upper right corner of the front flap with no ads for later titles.

Shaara, Michael. **The Killer Angels**. NY: MacKay, 1974. Copyright page has 5 lines of text on the top, and five lines of text on the bottom. The 5 lines on the top include the copyright year of 1974 and no other years nor any statement of subsequent printings. The 5 lines on the bottom include by-lines, identification numbers, and manufacturing information. Boards are light blue cloth with darker blue paper spine. 1st state dust jacket lacks reviews and a bar code.

Sidney, Margaret. **Five Little Peppers and How They Grew.** Boston: D. Lothrop & Company, 1880. In first issue the caption on page 231 is "said Polly"

Sinclair, Upton. **Dragon's Teeth**. NY: Viking, 1942. "FIRST PUBLISHED IN JANUARY 1942" on the verso with no other statements.
_____ **The Jungle**. New York: The Jungle Publishing Company, 1906. "Sustainer's Edition" is tipped into the first issue.

Singer, Isaac Bashevis. **A Crown of Feathers**. NY: Farrar, Strauss and Giroux, 1969. "First printing. 1973" is stated.

Siringo, Charles A. **Riata and Spurs**. Boston Houghton Mifflin Co. 1927. Original edition was suppressed by Pinkerton, later printings lack Pinkerton material.

Schlesinger, Arthur M. **A Thousand Days.** Boston: Houghton Mifflin, 1965. Limited edition, 1000 sigbed and numbered copies, of which 985 for sale. Full black and red leather binding, top edge gilt.

Smiley, Jane. **A Thousand Acres.** NY: Knopf. 1991. "First Edition" is stated.

Smith, Betty. **A Tree Grows in Brooklyn.** NY: Harper, 1943. FIRST EDITION is stated between codes "D-S" and "8-43". 1st issue dust jacket has code "5338".

Smith, E. E. **Grey Lensman.** Reading, PA.: Fantasy Press, 1951. Limited Edition of 500 Copies. First Edition Trade: Reading, PA.: Fantasy Press, 1951.The Gnome Press edition was printed with the Fantasy Press plates and states "First Edition," it is not.

Spock, Benjamin, M. D. **The Common Sense Book of Baby and Child Care.** NY: Duell, Sloan and Pierce, 1945. The print code on the title page is "1 2 3 4 5 CR 7595".

Stafford, Jean. **The Collected Stories of Jean Stafford.** NY: Farrar, Strauss and Giroux, 1969. "First printing" is stated.

Stegner, Wallace. **Angle of Repose.** Garden City, NY: Doubleday, 1971. "FIRST EDITION" is stated.
_____. **The Spectator Bird.** Franklin Center, PA: Franklin Library, 1988. Franklin Library "Limited First Edition."

Steinbeck, John. **Cannery Row.** NY: Viking, 1945. "First Published by The Viking Press in January 1945" is stated. First state has light-buff (tan) cloth boards and top page edge stained blue. Second state has yellow cloth boards.
_____. **East of Eden.** NY: Viking, 1952. Signed limited first edition of 1500 copies. 1st trade issue has 'bite' for 'bight' on page 281: line 38. 1st trade dust jacket has Steinbeck's photo with no blurbs.
_____. **The Grapes of Wrath.** NY: Viking, 1939. "FIRST PUBLISHED IN APRIL 1939" with no statement of subsequent printings. The Dust Jacket states "FIRST EDITION".
_____. **Of Mice and Men.** NY: Covici Friede, 1937. Contains misprints "and only moved because the heavy hands were pendula" on the bottom of page 9. There is also a bullet between the two 8's on the page number of page 88.
_____. **The Moon is Down.** New York: Viking, 1942. In first issue Page 112 line 11 has an extra period ""talk. this" and lacks a

mention of the printer (Haddon in later printings.)

_____. **The Pearl.** NY: Viking, 1939. "FIRST PUBLISHED BY THE VIKING PRESS IN DECEMBER 1947" with no statement of subsequent printings. 1st issue dust jacket has Steinbeck on the back panel looking toward his left (toward spine).

_____.**Travels with Charley in Search of America.** New York: The Viking Press, 1962. The first state dust jacket carries no mention of the Nobel Prize.

Stephenson, Neal. **Snow Crash.** NY: Bantam, 1992. Simultaneous Paperback and hardcover issue. Hardcover number line "FFG 9 8 7 6 5 4 3 2 1", maroon boards and dark blue cloth spine with silver lettering. 1st issue dust jacket has a reviews by William Gibson, Rudy Rucker, Timothy Leary, and James Morrow.

Stevens, Wallace. **Harmonium.** New York: Alfred A. Knopf, 1923. The first issue is bound in red, yellow, blue and white checkered boards.

_____. **The Man With The Blue Guitar & Other Poems.** New York: Alfred A. Knopf, 1937. The first state dustjacket has "conjunctioning" on the front flap.

Stevenson, Robert Lewis. **David Balfour: Being Memoirs of his Adventure at Home and Abroad.** London: Cassell, 1893. First Issue has the following points: page 40,line 11 "business"; page 64, line 1 "nine o"clock"; page 101, line 10 "Islands"; as well as the rear ads dated "5.G.4.86" and "5.B.4.86."

Stockton, Frank R. **The Casting Away of Mrs. Lecks and Mrs. Aleshine.** New York: Century Co., 1886. The signatures are numbered on Pp. 9, 25, 49, 57, 73, 81, 97, 105, 121 and 125 in the first issue.

Stone, Robert. **Dog Soldiers**. Boston: Houghton-Mifflin, 1974. FIRST PRINTING stated.

Stowe, Harriet Beecher. **Uncle Tom's Cabin.** Boston & Cleveland, OH: John P. Jewett & Co. & Jewett, Proctor and Worthington, 1852. (Two Volumes). The second printing carries "ten thousand" on the title page.

Stribling, Thomas. **The Store.** Garden City, NY: Doubleday Doran, 1932. "FIRST EDITION" is stated on bottom of copyright page. Title page states MCMXXXII (1932 - the original publication year). Black cloth with illustrated label on front cover and on spine.

Strout, Elizabeth. **Olive Kitteridge**. NY: Random House, 2008. Number line is "9 8 7 6 5 4 3 2 1".

Styron, William. **The Confessions of Nat Turner.** NY: Random House, 1967. "First Printing" is stated black cloth with silver lettering, brown/maroon top stain, price of $6.95 is found on the upper right corner of the front dust jacket flap, and "10/67" at the bottom. 500 copies of the first edition were printed on special paper, bound in red cloth with silver lettering over black on the spine, and issued in an orange slip case, signed and numbered.

Susann, Jacqueline. **The Valley of the Dolls**. NY: Bernard Geis, 1966. First Printing stated.

Tan. Amy. **The Joy Luck Club.** NY: Putnam, 1989. Number line "1 2 3 4 5 6 7 8 9 10". Boards are gray with blue/green spine. 1st issue dust jacket is priced $18.95 with $26.50 Canadian beneath, three review blurbs by Alice Walker, Alice Hoffman, and Louise Erdrich.

Tarkington, Booth. **Alice Adams.** Garden City, NY: Doubleday, Page, 1921. "you" and "why" are transposed on page 419, line 14. It reads "I can't see you why don't wear more colour,..."
_____. **The Magnificent Ambersons.** Garden City, NY: Doubleday, Page, 1918. Rust red boards stamped in black. Title page and copyright page should both say 1918 with no other statement of printings.

Taylor, Peter. **A Summons to Memphis.** NY: Knopf, 1986. "First Edition" is stated.

Taylor, Robert Lewis. **The Travels of Jamie Mcpheeters.** Garden City, NY: Doubleday, 1958. "First Edition" is stated.

Thompson, Ruth Plumly. **The Royal Book of Oz.** Chicago: Reilly and Lee, 1921. First state has a typo "scarecorws" on page 255.
_____.**Grampa in Oz.** Chicago: Reilly and Lee, 1924. First state has perfect type on pages 171 and 189.
_____.**The Lost King of Oz.** Chicago: Reilly and Lee, 1925. Serif is unbroken on the k in line 4 on page 193 of the first issue.
_____.**The Hungry Tiger of Oz.** Chicago: Reilly and Lee, 1926. First state has a hyphen on the last line of page 21 and the word "two" in perfect type on the last line of page 252.
_____.**The Giant Horse of Oz.** Chicago: Reilly and Lee, 1928. A damaged 'r' in 'morning' on p. 116 line 1. and frontispiece misprint 'Oniberon' for 'Quiberon' in first issue.

Thoreau, Henry David. **A Week On The Concord And Merrimac Rivers.** Boston and Cambridge: James Munroe, 1849. Basically vanity published, Thoreau got most of the first printing cut and gathered binding as they sold over a number of years so the bindings vary widely.

Tolkien, J.R. R. **The Hobbitt**. George Allen & Unwin, 1937. FIRST PUBLISHED IN 1937 is stated with no references to subsequent printings. First issue dust jacket has Dodgeson misspelt on bottom of rear flap, usually corrected in ink by hand.

Toole, John Kennedy. **A Confederacy of Dunces.** Baton Rouge: Louisiana State University Press, 1980. Matching dates of 1980 on the title page and verso with no references to a other printings. 1st issue of the dust jacket has Walker Percy's blurb on the rear with no other blurbs.

Trollope, Anthony. **Prime Minister.** London: Chapman & Hall, 1876. First edition in the eight monthly parts: brown cloth-cased with original printed wrappers bound in.

Truman, Harry S. **Mr. Citizen.** NY: Bernard Geis, New York, 1960. A signed limited edition in publisher slipcase.

Tuck, Lily. **The News from Paraguay.** NY: HarperCollins, 2004. FIRST EDITION stated with number lines "04 05 06 07 08" and "10 9 8 7 6 5 4 3 2 1".

Twain, Mark. **A Tramp Abroad.** Hartford: American Publishing Company, 1880. Cover blind stamped border and the frontespice is labled "Moses".
_____. **The Adventures of Huckleberry Finn**. London: Chatto and Windus, 1884.
Frist U.S. Edition: New York: Charles L. Webster and Co., 1885. At p. 13 the erroneous page reference 88 was changed to 87; at p. 57 the misprint with the was corrected to "with the saw"; and at p. 9 the misprint Decided was corrected to "Decides" in later editions.
_____. **The Celebrated Jumping Frog of Calaveras County.** New York: C. H. Webb, 1867. Ads precede title page in first issue "life" is unbroken in the last line of page 66 and "this" is unbroken in the last line on page 198.
_____. **Life on the Mississippi.** Chatto & Windus, 1883 First US Edition: Boston: James R. Osgood And Co., 1883. Page 411 tail-piece with urn, flames and head of Twain; page 443 caption reads "The St. Louis Hotel."
_____. **Punch, Brothers, Punch! and Other Sketches.** New York: Slote, Woodman, 1878. The title page of the first issue had "Mark Twain" in roman type.
_____. **Roughing it.** Hartford: American Publishing Company, 1872. Page xi, line "My perfect", page 242, lines 20-21 "premises-said he/was occupying his..." in first issue.   .

Tyler, Anne. **Breathing Lessons.** Franklin Center, PA: Franklin Library, 1988. Franklin Library "Signed First Edition."
_____. **If Morning Ever Comes.** New York: Alfred A. Knopf, 1964. "than" in quote on front flap of first issue dust jacket.

Updike, John. **The Centaur**. NY: Knopf, 1963. FIRST EDITION stated, cream color boards with black cloth spine and red topstain. 1st issue dust jacket back has reviews for *The Poorhouse Fair; The Same Door; Rabbit, Run*; and *Pigeon Features*.

_____. **Rabbit at Rest.** Franklin Center, PA: Franklin Library, 1988. Franklin Library "Signed First Edition."

_____. **Rabbit is Rich.** NY: Knopf, 1981. Limited edition of 350 copies signed and numbered. The first trade edition which states "FIRST EDITION".

Van Dyne, S. S. **The Benson Murder Case.** New York: Charles Scribners, 1926. Roman numerals on title page (MCMXXVI) and "copyright 1926" on copyright page with Scribner's seal. "Canary Murder Case" noted "in Preparation".

_____. **The Canary Murder Case.** New York: Charles Scribners, 1927. Roman numerals on title page (MCMXXVII) and "copyright 1927" on copyright page with Scribner's seal. "Taxicab Murder Case" noted "in Preparation".

_____. **The Greene Murder Case.** New York: Charles Scribners, 1928. Roman numerals on title page (MCMXXVIII) and "copyright 1928" on copyright page with Scribner's seal. "Mother Goose Murder Case" noted "in Preparation".

_____. **The Bishop Murder Case.** New York: Charles Scribners, 1929. Roman numerals on title page (MCMXXIX) and "copyright 1929" on copyright page with Scribner's seal. "Scarab Murder Case" noted "in Preparation".

Vollmann, William. **Europe Central.** NY: Viking, 2005. "First published in 2005 by Viking Penguin stated with number line "10 9 8 7 6 5 4 3 2 1"

Vonnegut, Kurt. **Player Piano.**New York: Scribners, 1952. First state has both Scribner's "A" and colophon on the verso.

_____. **Slaughterhouse-Five.** NY: Delacorte, 1969. First Printing is stated 1st issue dust jacket price is priced $5.95.

Walker, Alice. **The Color Purple**. NY: Harcourt, 1982. States "First Edition" and the letter code "BCDE".

Wallace, Lew. **Ben-Hur. A Tale of the Christ.** New York: Harper & Brothers, 1880. The first issue has a misprint on page 11 line 37 "be-became" and a two line dedication "To/ The Wife of My Youth", changed to "To/ The Wife of My Youth/ Who Still Abides with Me" in later editions.

Wambaugh, Joseph. **The New Centurions.** Boston: Little Brown, 1970. Nearly identical with book club editions the true first has no detent (small blind stamp) on the rear board.

_____. **The Onion Field.** NY: Delacorte, 1973. "First

printing 1973" is stated. 1st issue dust jacket carries a single review by Truman Capote.

Warhol, Andy **The Index Book.** New York: Random House, 1967. Issued with 1) colored pop-up castle 2) folding page with paper accordion 3) "The Chelsea Girls" paper disc.; 4) colored pop-up airplane 4) mobile on a piece of black string 5) flexi-disc of the Velvet Underground illustrated with a portrait of Lou Reed 6) folding illustration of a nose 7) colored pop-up Hunt's Tomato Paste Cans 8) Inflatable sponge 9) balloon 10) tear-out postcard

Warren, Robert Penn. **All the King's Men.** NY: Harcourt, 1946. "first edition" is stated on the verso, 1st state dustjacket has Sinclair Lewis blurb on the back.

Watson, James. **The Double Helix.** NY: Atheneum, 1968. First Edition is stated. 1st issue dust Jacket back has photo of the author in Paris with reviews below.

Wells, H.G. **The Time Machine.** London: William Heinemann, 1895. First Edition binding grey stamped in purple with 16 pages of ads.
_____. **The Island of Doctor Moreau.** London, William Heinemann, 1896. The first issue has 32 pages of ads at the end.
_____. **The Invisible Man.** London: C. Arthur Pearson, 1897. Page 1 labeled 2 in first state.
_____. **The War of the Worlds.** London, William Heinemann, 1898. 16 pp of advertisements at end.
_____. *The First Men in the Moon.* Indianapolis: Bowen-Merrill Company, 1901. First UK Edition: London: George Newnes, 1901. Original issue is dark blue cloth stamped in gilt. Strand Magazine 1900-01 (four volumes), first appearances of *First Men in the Moon* and A.C.Doyle's The *Hound of the Baskervilles*

Welty, Eudora. **The Optimist's Daughter**. NY: Random House, 1972. a limited edition of no more than 300 numbered copies signed. First trade edition "FIRST EDITION " is stated over the line 9 8 7 6 5 4 3 2.

Wharton, Edith. **The Age of Innocence.** NY: D. Appleton, 1920. Has "(1)" on the last page of text, which indicates it is the first printing.

White, Stewart Edward. **Gold.** Garden City, NY: Doubleday Page, 1913. First Issue is bound in yellow.

Wilder, Laura Ingalls. **Little House on the Prairie.** NY: Harper, 1941. First Edition stated with Harper code "K-Q".

Wilder, Thornton. **The Eighth Day**. NY: Harper, 1972. "First Edition" stated, light blue cloth with black cloth spine with gold lettering. 1st state dust jacket has code "0367".

Williams, John. **Augustus**. NY: Viking, 1964. States "First published in 1972 by the Viking Press, Inc." Brick-red boards with green cloth spine. 1st issue dust jacket has one review by Orville Prescott.

Willams, Thomas. **The Hair of Harold Roux**. NY: Random House, 1974. FIRST EDITION is stated with number line "24689753", maroon with boards gold lettering. 1st issue dust jacket has no reviews.

Williams, William Carlos. **A beginning on the short story.** Yonkers, NY: The Alicat Bookshop Press, 1950. Known to go beyond stated 750 copy limit, binding varies, cream and tan, priority unknown.

Wilson, Margaret. **The Able McLaughlins.** NY: Harper, 1923. "First Edition" and H-X (August 1923) on verso.

Wodehouse P.G. **The Pothunters.** London: Adam and Charles Black, 1902. There are no advertisements in the first state.
_____. **Louder and Funnier.** London: Faber and Faber, 1932. First Issue is red cloth with black lettering, copyright date in roman numerals.
_____.**The Man with Two Left Feet.** London: Methuen, 1917. First Issue is gold/yellow cloth with gold lettering.
_____.**My Man Jeeves.**: George Newnes, 1919.
First Issue is red cloth with black lettering.
_____.**The Inimitable Jeeves.** London: Herbert Jenkins, 1923. First issue has 13 titles of Jenkins books ending with "The Coming of Bill"
_____.**Carry On Jeeves.** London: Herbert Jenkins, 1925. First Issue is green cloth with black lettering with title page dated in roman numerals.
_____. **Very Good Jeeves.** Garden City, NY: Doubleday Doran, 1930. First UK Edition: London: Herbert Jenkins, 1930. First Issue is orange cloth with black lettering.
_____. **Thank You, Jeeves.** London: Herbert Jenkins, 1934. First Issue is gray cloth with red lettering.
_____.*Right Ho, Jeeves.*
First Edition: London: Herbert Jenkins, 1934.
Nr.Fine/Fine $1400. Good/V.Good $400.
Points of Issue: First Issue is grey cloth with red lettering, title page date is in roman numerals.
First US Edition as *Brinkley Manor*: Boston: Little Brown, 1934.
_____. **The Code of the Woosters.** London: Herbert Jenkins, 1938. First Issue is green cloth with black lettering & decorations.
_____. **The Mating Season**. Herbert Jenkins, 1949. First Issue is orange cloth with black lettering.
_____.**Ring for Jeeves.** London: Herbert Jenkins, 1953. First Issue is red cloth with black lettering.
_____. **Jeeves and the Feudal Spirit.** London: Herbert Jenkins, 1954.

First Issue is red cloth with black lettering.

_____. **A Few Quick Ones**. London: Herbert Jenkins, 1959. First Issue is red cloth with black lettering.

_____. **Jeeves in the Offing.** London: Herbert Jenkins, 1960.: First Issue is red cloth with gold lettering.

_____. **Stiff Upper Lip, Jeeves.** London: Herbert Jenkins, 1963. First Issue is red buckram with gold lettering.

_____. **Plum Pie.** London: Herbert Jenkins, 1966. First Issue is purple cloth with silver lettering.

_____. **Much Obliged, Jeeves.** London: Barrie & Jenkins, 1971. First Issue is blue cloth with gold lettering. Nr.Fine/Fine $125. Good/V.Good $50.

_____. **Aunts Aren't Gentlemen.** London: Barrie & Jenkins, 1974. First Issue is blue cloth with gold lettering and decorations

Wolfe, Tom. **The Bonfire of the Vanities.** Franklin Center, PA: Franklin Library, 1987. Franklin Library "Signed First Edition."

_____. **The Right Stuff.** NY: Farrar, Strauss and Giroux, 1979. "First printing, 1979" is stated with gray boards.

Wolfe, Thomas. **Look Homeward, Angel.** New York: Charles Scribner's Sons, 1929. Dust jacket carries a picture of Wolfe and the verso has a Scribner's colophon in first issue.

Wolfram, Stephen. **A New Kind of Science**. Champaign, Il: Wolfram Media, 2002. "First edition. First printing" is stated.

Wouk, Herman. **The Caine Mutiny**. Garden City, NY: Doubleday, 1951. "First Edition" is stated on the verso. 1st state dust Jacket that says "The City Boy" on the back cover.

Wright, Richard. **Black Boy.** New York and London: Harper & Brothers, 1945. Stated First Edition with code M-T 1st issue dust jacket- $2.50 price, "5760" on front flap, "5761" on back flap, and "No.2209" on back cover of jacket.

Wyndham, John. **The Day of the Triffids.** London: Michael Joseph, 1951. First Issue has an advertising band stating "The Daily Graphic Book Find of the Month".

14524456R00094

Made in the USA
Lexington, KY
04 April 2012